THE SIMPLICITY OF
THE VIOLIN

THE SIMPLICITY OF PLAYING THE VIOLIN

by

HERBERT WHONE

With illustrations by the author
and a preface by
COLIN DAVIS

LONDON
VICTOR GOLLANCZ LTD
1980

First published 1972
This edition 1980

ISBN 0 575 02753 3

Printed in Great Britain by
St Edmundsbury Press Limited, Haverhill, Suffolk

Dedicated with gratitude to
my first and last teachers
H. H.
and
E. H.

ACKNOWLEDGEMENTS

To all who have contributed to my understanding of the violin and of life: to the friends who have offered stylistic criticism: to my son Adam who posed for the drawings, and to my wife and other children who saw little of me during the time of its writing: and finally to my students of the last few years without whom I would have learnt nothing.

H. W.

CONTENTS

PREFACE

IF A BOOK devoted to so specialised a subject as the study of a musical instrument is to be more than a list of instructions, the writer must be aware of the wider implications of his own specialised technique: he must have read, studied and experienced and have applied his hard won knowledge first to himself and then to those for whom he is responsible as a teacher. Fortunately for us Herbert Whone is such a man: a fine violinist and a painter besides, he has, in the interests of a broader view of life, eschewed professional ambition and devoted himself to discovering a deeper understanding of what, besides the use of arms and fingers, is involved in the mastery of the violin.

He knows for example that a teacher must spend most of his time disentangling the complexities of the human machine, studying the three aspects of man's being, mind, body and heart and understanding the functions of each separately before finding the harmony in which they can work without mutual interference. The interference with this harmony usually shows itself in unnecessary tension in the muscles and in the inability to attend to the matter in hand for more than a few moments: energy is in fact going to waste through what we have come to regard as the natural inefficiency of most of us, and it is only through a prolonged apprenticeship of self-observation under the right teacher that we begin to notice how inefficient our energy system really is.

The aspect of Herbert Whone's book which strikes me as the most stimulating is that he relates all the technical problems of playing the violin to the view that even if man is not made in

God's image, he is at least made in the image of this fallen universe and is subject to its laws; laws that man can learn to use to his own advantage by observing how they operate round him and by applying them to his own tripartite structure. In particular he makes imaginative use of the interplay of the opposite forces within and without us; the two contraries which are as necessary to the development of the human spirit as two wings are to the flight of a bird. In the mastery of any skill these forces may be exploited consciously; unfortunately most of our time is spent in suffering from them unconsciously because we are unable to stand back sufficiently far from ourselves to see their operation in all we do.

Looked at in this way the study of a musical instrument can teach us much about ourselves that we ought to know and if we follow the author's advice in applying that knowledge to all our activities we shall find, in practicing a skill, a true education that far transcends the isolated activity of learning to play notes. If the purpose of our lives is to develop to the full the powers within us, then this book may well set the feet of many students upon that way: the only way that makes true sense of all our efforts.

COLIN DAVIS

INTRODUCTION

ALTHOUGH THE subject of this book is a highly complex one, I have entitled it *The Simplicity of Playing the Violin*. This is because underlying apparent complexity lies a fundamental simplicity which has the power to make light of so-called problems and difficulties. Mastery in any field of activity can only be attained by reaching as far back as possible through complexity to this simplicity.

A musicologist may analyse a piece of music down to the last demi-semiquaver but fail ever to relive the original creative experience of the composer; a doctor may treat complex symptoms of an illness in the physical body and fail to relate them to a deeper and more subtle source; or in the teaching of mathematics, unless the exact meaning of a question can be conveyed, a child will struggle with figures to no avail. It is the same for the violinist. Unless he understands the simple principles upon which a complex technique is built, his playing will be insecure and unreliable.

This book has been written therefore in an attempt to understand violin playing from its deepest roots. It is not intended merely to restate technical issues—nor is it in any way intended to belittle great schools of the violin, but rather to analyse the principles that underlie any efficient technique. These principles do not relate solely to violin playing: they are universal principles to be found in fields of activity and teachings as far apart as archery, Jungian psychology, tight-rope walking or the Tao Te Ching. All have the same end—that delicate balance between spirit and matter in which the body is a willing servant of the spirit and in which its laws of gravity are transcended.

It is for this reason that so much initial stress has been laid on the releasing of all tensions and blockages to freedom in the limbs. The body can be likened to a great machine working with such precision that one marvels how such opposites can co-exist in the same operation. Very few violinists achieve this balance of opposites. The sorry fact is that they have been taught to play before they have been made aware of their bodies, and the perfect control of the limbs which should be at the basis of their technique has scarcely ever been considered.

There are those who say that to impose rules upon different individuals is wrong, and that a student should be encouraged to play in his own natural way. In very rare cases this may be so, but more often than not, the natural way is evasive of real issues and is only interested in comfort. Comfort yields to the gravity pulls of the body and retards rather than hastens development. Moreover, as we can see elsewhere in life, efficiency depends upon rules of mechanics: most bridges remain standing because these rules have been observed. Many violinists fail because the necessity for a scientific study of mechanics has not been understood. It is also said that too unrelenting a method produces machines and not individual players. There is no intention here to turn out computored violinists. What is intended is that a basic and universal logic should be understood in order later that individual characteristics may flourish. Every individual has his own particular identity within the universal scheme, and for this reason allowance has always to be made in teaching for the modification of rules—but this does not mean we can dispose of first principles: an individual branch still owes its life to universal roots.

In presenting this book, I address myself to all violinists, whom I will take the liberty of dividing into three categories: students and amateurs, professionals, and teachers of the young.

The hope is that it may encourage students and amateurs to work upon habits which are a hindrance to progress, spark off a new interest for professionals in an instrument which they might long ago have taken for granted, and help teachers of the young to be aware of the truth that physical difficulties need never occur if the child is trained in the use of his body from the very beginning.

The order of presentation in the book is roughly as though a beginner were studying problems for the first time, but this is only in the interests of logical shape and should not preclude the interest of the advanced player. The basic initial ideas soon overlap and inter-penetrate later aspects of technique and other matters of wider interest. The intention has been not to produce an orthodox manual of the violin but to present some basic concepts which may prove stimulating to violinists at all levels.

THE SIMPLICITY OF PLAYING
THE VIOLIN

I

FEELING AWARENESS IN THE BODY

THE PHYSICAL freedom upon which a healthy technique depends is not easily acquired. The body is taken for granted and real *feeling awareness* of it is seldom experienced. By *feeling awareness* is meant the ability of the body to sense its own existence—for the body to be conscious of itself. It is not sufficient to talk of being more aware of the body because this suggests simply observing it from the outside, and we are referring to the possibility of feeling from within. The difficulty arises because a human being generally spends his life in a state of identification with the external world which dulls sensitivity at all levels of his being. On one level his consciousness itself is limited; he is aware as an animal, but not aware that he is aware—a reflexive capacity that differentiates him from an animal: and on the level that concerns us in this chapter, he uses his body, but in such a mechanical way that he scarcely knows that it exists. It would be true to say, in fact, that when it is not suffering pain, the body is more often than not blind to itself.

It is because of this blindness that tensions creep into the muscles and joints of a man's body during his life, interfering with his natural freedom of movement. To recover this freedom should be the first aim of all students of the violin, because there is no activity which requires more sensitivity of control, more speed of action, or more power of attack, than the arms and fingers of a violinist.

To do this may take a considerable amount of time and training. It is surprising how reluctant a student is to accept that there is anything wrong with his body, and how difficult it is to persuade him to spend time on what seems to him an unimportant matter. He may be quite convinced, for example, that his right arm is relaxed, and yet it may be necessary to press with considerable force to bring it down from a playing position to his side. In the same way, if two long notes are played, say the open E followed by the open G, he may be unaware that

towards the end of the E an antici- patory tension has arisen in his arm inhibiting a free and rapid movement across the string. The teacher, how- ever, by putting his hand on the bow arm, can easily feel this tension and indicate to the pupil the moment when it begins to arise. Or, at any time during playing, the fingers of the left hand may have become so contracted that they have to be prised forcibly off the string. These are the sort of instances that can show a student the extent to which muscular contractions have limited his playing.

Contraction is a violinist's chief enemy. It is, as the word suggests, contra-action, against action, and to realise this is the key to control in the body. In saying this, however, we have to be careful to understand that contraction is a relative term: for playing to be possible or even for an arm simply to be held out from the body, some degree of contraction or tension is neces- sary. But this is minimal and does not overstep the bounds of economic necessity. The contraction referred to as an enemy is in excess of what is necessary and is a hindrance to action.

But it is not easy for a student to know if he has succeeded in reaching that point of minimal tension which allows him the greatest possible freedom of movement, because, as we have said, he may have little ability to sense his own body. If this is felt to be the case, there are a number of ways in which he may be helped, but the following two are perhaps the most effica- cious.

In the first, he may sit quietly without external distraction

(preferably with the eyes shut), and, eliminating normal thinking processes, try to isolate in sensation different parts of the
body. It is a help initially to gently move or touch a specific
part so as to locate it, but the aim is to be aware of the actual
life movement within say a finger or an elbow. This sensing of
life within the body is the feeling awareness of the title of the
chapter. Its inherent difficulty is that it cannot be described—
only experienced, but it must be sought, because without it
contraction cannot even be identified let alone released.

In the second, he may make himself increasingly aware of
what contraction is—the method of knowing a thing by its
opposite. Either arm is held out in its approximate position for
playing and the muscles tightened until they are rigid. This
produces immobility in the arm. The grip is then released and
an attempt made to feel the opposite state of lightness. As the
grip is released there is a gradual increase in mobility until the
arm finally feels able to move freely and at speed in any direction. The return to the contracted state is then made immediately and an alternation between the two states kept up so that
the difference between them can be keenly registered. For some
this exercise may be difficult and at first the extreme may not be
fully reached, but by moving between one and the other,
familiarity with them may be developed and their limits
extended. The exercise can be extended by increasing sensitivity
to different degrees of tension between the extremes. To do this
it is useful to draw upon images of corresponding density from
the natural world. Maximum contraction could for instance be
imaged as steel, and minimum contraction as air, and between
them in descending order the different degrees of density could
be imaged as stone, soil, wood, water and paper. The middle
degrees of this seven-fold scale would then correspond to the
tension states that normally inhabit and inhibit the body during
waking life and in the practice room. By becoming familiar with
such states at the shoulder, elbows and wrists, it is possible to

control and ultimately transform them at will into the air state. The air state is our objective and cannot be stressed too much: it is only from this state that the bow can be sensitively controlled. As we shall see in a later chapter, the bow arm is only efficient when it moves into action from a state of minimal tension and can return to that state at will.

This feeling awareness is then the basis for all control of the body and must be seen as the first stage in a player's training. It does not apply only to the arms, though of course they are of primary importance: in the act of playing, all parts of the body interrelate and a lockage in one place is felt in the others. The lightness of air should extend to every limb and muscle in the body until it is felt as a totally flexible unit. The delicate interplay of stress and strain within the body is to do with stance and balance which will be discussed in the next chapter.

2

STANCE AND BALANCE

IT IS UNFORTUNATE that the violin has to be played at all in the sitting position. Balance is restricted by the body being severed half-way down and a player often feels the need to rise and avail himself of his whole strength: leaders of orchestras faced with difficult solos know this feeling well. But even in the relatively free standing position the problem of balance needs close attention. Many players give the impression of suffering from some muscular paralysis and there is an instability which in some cases is so pronounced that a mere push on the arm can cause the body to lose balance completely.

For this to be possible, the joints and muscles of both arms and legs must be so severely locked as to deny the possibility of movement: it is movement that is the key to balance and only through movement can such a tendency to overbalance be countered. The push could be absorbed in the arm by yielding at the shoulder and the elbow, and in the legs by flexible movement at the joints which allows counter-balancing to take place. (This is a technique of defence well known in the art of Judo.) In all fields, in fact, stability lies in movement and not in a deceptively secure-looking immobility. Upon this principle a juggler keeps his plates revolving on top of a stick, and a tight-rope walker keeps his balance. A child's top, giving the illusion of stillness at the moment of its greatest movement, illustrates even more clearly that dynamic stability equals movement.

The equivalent movement that gives the violinist his stability is an alternative transferring of the weight of the body from foot to foot whilst he plays. This movement, however sensitive it may be, is a condition of balance and depends entirely upon the placing of the feet. An incorrect placing of the feet destroys

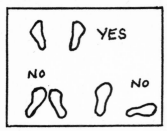

balance. If they are too close together, the body is liable to over-balance; on the other hand if they are too wide apart the body becomes unyielding— movement is restricted; or if the right foot is turned out at too much of an angle, there is an awkward tension in the leg which affects the whole feeling in the body. And so on. Inefficient positions of the feet are legion.

Their most efficient position is about a foot apart and facing slightly outwards, though the distance is modifiable according to the weight and height of the player. This allows the freest and most natural alternation of weight to take place from foot to foot. Within this general indication it is up to each player to experiment and develop the balance that works most naturally for him. If there is no stability in the feet, all that lies above will feel equally insecure, and the significance of this for the violinist need not be stressed.

An erect spine is also an important factor in balance. It will be found that if the spine bends forward at the waist, again the sense of free movement and balance is inhibited. Meditative postures have long ago recognised the significance of the well aligned spine to the harmonious functioning of both inner powers and outer body. It is equally important for the violinist. But erectness does not signify rigidity and the spine must be flexible throughout its length: the rigidity imposed by such disciplines as the army is harmful to health and has no place here. In fact the spine, as the diagram illustrates is not literally erect—it has its own natural way of carrying the weight of the body, and all that is asked is that this should be allowed to happen without strain. Flexibility is particularly necessary at the root of the spine. Simple exercises freeing any contraction there are a help—twisting the whole trunk, bending forward as though bowing or leaning from right to left as though passing a heavy bucket from hand to hand. Within this total flexibility the aim should be for the upper part of the body to sit securely balanced on the pelvis without any sensation of its being pulled forward.

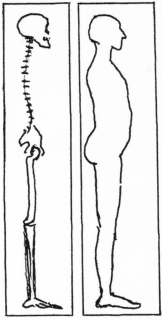

Another point about spinal alignment is that the head scarcely ever sits well; there is a tendency for it to droop forward, causing tensions in the neck and shoulder muscles. In this and in the whole question of balance, awareness of the 'atlas' bone, the topmost bone in the spinal column and so named because it bears the skull or world of the individual, is extremely valuable. If at the same time as maintaining flexibility in the erect spine, the head is slightly raised until its actual point of balance between the ears is sensed, the body can be released of much of its weight and a perfect sense of balance can be achieved. This of course is without the instrument—initial exercises are best restricted to the body alone. When the violin is held despite the fact that certain pressures are called into play, this ideal should be approximated as closely as possible.

It goes without saying, too, that in the sitting position, which is the lot of most violinists, the same general principles apply. An indication of a good sitting position can be gained by the ease with which it is possible to move immediately from the chair to the feet, for the transition, in terms of energy expenditure, is negligible if the sitting position is alive and alert. Because we are sitting it does not excuse us from the need to use our bodies sensitively: the concepts of *balance*, *erectness*, and *flexibility* should always be borne in mind.

All these aspects of stance and balance can now be combined. Like a scientifically designed bridge, which, though of the slenderest appearance is able to carry a great weight of traffic, so the body well rooted in mechanical laws will safely carry the superstructure of a complex technique.

3

HOLDING THE VIOLIN—THE LAW OF RIGHT-OVER-LEFT

WHEN VIOLIN and bow are held in a playing position, the findings about stance and balance of the last chapter need to be qualified. The right and left sides have now to be seen as having different functions. On the right hand the bow initiates the expenditure of energy, and on the left hand the violin receives that expended energy. Right acts upon left. To understand this relationship of violin and bow, the symbolic meaning of right and left requires a little consideration.

Most major religions of the world contain the concept that the process of bringing the world into being involves the enclosing of the power of the creator. That is to say that once enclosed, power has lost its singleness and become a duality—it is both *outside* and *inside*. In a sense power can then be said to have died because it is then only free to act within the laws that govern a particular life-form. From this division of power have arisen all erroneous dualistic concepts. God and the Devil, for instance, are seen as separate forces, whereas seen as *deus inversus* the Devil is simply the other face of God. In man, that enclosing process is the condition of his own self-consciousness and his self-willing, so that he has a free side and a bound side—a so-called good and a so-called evil side to his nature. The good wishes to acknowledge and return to the sources of his origin and the evil desires to remain separate and isolated from it.

Or this fundamental division can be seen in another light—that of the conflict between will and reason. The question of which came first has long been disputed by philosophers. Those who acknowledge the superiority of will do so because, they say, will is essentially unconditioned, and in the conceiving of the idea and in the precipitation of that idea as form, it has made a limit upon its own unconditioned nature. Whichever way it is seen, we have the same idea of division—a free power and the same power that has limited itself. It is in the opposition between these two forces that the drama of the cosmos lies.

Now man is described by the ancients, and for that matter by many current teachings, as a microcosmos (small universe), in which all that is in the macrocosmos (great universe), is inevitably bound. In this light a man's outer form is merely the expression of universal principles, and he has only to look within himself to find these principles at work. Thus, in the particular issue we are discussing, it is the conflict between the free and the enclosed and between will and reason which has some correspondence with the right-left division in his physical body. Of the many indications of this in life, only a few can be given here. The word *left* itself is said to derive from either Old English or Latin roots, both of which have a similar meaning— *infirm* and *death* respectively; and the Latin word for left (*sinistra*) is clearly related to the English *sinister*. The human face itself has a left side and a right side, a fact well known to portrait painters who look to the left side for the cold and calculating, and to the right side for the warm and wilful in the personality. In ballet, the drama of man's duality is expressed by the symbolic entry of the evil force from the left and the good force from the right. The significance of the word *right* is reflected in right, meaning the opposite of wrong, and the executive power of man lies in his right arm.

These examples are only a few out of a great number that would make absorbing material for study. But how does all this relate to the violinist as he holds the bow in the right hand and the violin in the left? Has he ever considered this simple fact to be part of the drama of existence? For him, it is clearly a question of deputing authority to the correct side. For left to be over right—for the violin to dominate the bow in any way— would mean the reversal of a natural order in which weakness would be set up over strength. It is for this reason that the bow, from the very beginning, should be trained to be in a position of command over the violin. The whole picture, both as regards stance and the way the instrument is held, should be determined by this basic concept.

To see how this works in practice, let us first consider a few well known violin holds in which efficiency is impaired by the reversal of the rule. In position A where the violin is held out too far to the left, the bow has an obvious struggle to assume authority: it neither feels nor looks to be in command. Nor can it move in a straight line with the bridge, which is a pre-condition of pure tone. Firmness of tone is impossible from such a position.

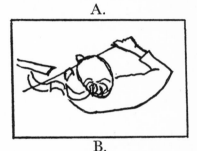

A.

When held too high in the air, as in position B, the violin dominates the bow. From this position, weight can not be applied adequately, and the bow moves ineffectually over the strings giving a thin tone.

B.

If the angle of the violin is steep, as in position C, the arm is too close to the side to be able to command the instrument. There is a sense of restriction in the movement of the arm, and the fingers compensate by gripping the bow. The result is a thin hard tone.

C.

In position D where the head

D.

perches vertically on a flat instrument, the whole area, except for the hand, lies below the plane of the strings. Again the bow is made subservient to the violin, and the fingers controlling the pressure produce an anaemic tone.

All these positions create the same deficiency of tone through a wrong right-left relationship: the angles clearly need adjustment to give a relationship in which the bow adequately commands the instrument. The suggestions that follow, however, are only to be regarded as a broad framework for experiment; individual physical differences have always to be considered. In position A, the angle should be adjusted so that the violin is no more than 30° off centre; in position B the violin should be lowered until it is fractionally under parallel to the ground; in position C, the tilt should be adjusted to about 20° from parallel; and in position D, the angle of C should be

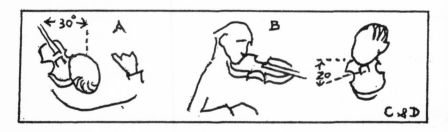

adopted and the head inclined to the left to make it more of a unit with the violin. If these adjustments are combined successfully, the result will be a hold which satisfies the needs of a right-left relationship and to which all other issues to do with holding the violin should be referred.

Unfortunately, because this question is not considered with care, and due to the peculiarities of jaw and collar bones, the violin is often held quite arbitrarily. Attempts to remedy physical peculiarities by shoulder rests—which term covers anything from elegant commercial lines to home-made pads— only meet with moderate success, for, without a basic concept from which to work, the shoulder rest simply determines the angles at which the violin is held: and it is scientifically proven angles that should determine the shape and nature of the rest. Equally a dogmatic attitude about not using a rest often causes much trouble. A wrongly chosen rest can throw the violin up high as in position B, cause it to slide sloppily down onto the chest, or set it at an exaggerated angle as in position C: it is the cause of many ills. As for chin-rests, though they are often a cause of irritation, they do not affect the hold of the violin so much: with the head slightly inclined to the left, the aim should be to find a rest that as far as possible fits the line of the jaw. An indication of success in this problem of shoulder and chin rests is if the head and instrument can be felt as one secure unit without the necessity for gripping by the chin, and yet held in such a way as to give the appearance of being sculpted from the same block of wood. Until such time in the future when a work- able system may have been evolved for measuring violinists as a bespoke tailor measures his client, a player can only make his own experiments along the lines suggested.

The right-left principle can now be carried through into the whole body. The important thing is that the weight of the body should be felt on the left foot, and that the left side, relative to the right, should be static. This does not mean to say there is a permanently heavy or rigid lean to the left; as we have seen, balance depends upon alternations of stress between right and left. It means that there is a continual return to the left foot as the bow assumes its authoritative role over the instrument. 'Dynamically static' best describes the left side, since it involves the images of stillness and movement in one. The weight of the body should never fall heavily on the right foot—nor should there be any lean to the right: this raises the violin above the

bow-arm which is then unable to attack effectively. The opening of the Brahms Concerto, for instance, cannot be made with weight on the right foot: force can only be applied adequately with the weight of the body firmly on the left foot and the bow-arm in a position of command over the instrument.

Although this rule about the left side should be generally observed in playing, there is one modification that can be suggested in the interests of a sensitive relationship between the body and the shaping of the music. If weight is transferred from the left to the right foot, but the head is kept in line above the

left foot, a slight curve is produced in the body. This has the effect of flattening the angle of the violin and of raising the bow-arm from the side so that right commands left despite the transference of the weight of the body to the right foot. During playing, there is a correspondence between this movement and emphasis in phrasing or dynamics. In as sensitive a lift, for instance, as that between the last two notes in this theme from the Bartok *Roumanian Dances*, a slight movement from a

central balance to the bend at the waist (as in the diagram), allows the bow to exert the most gentle of stresses. In more intense phrasing, as in the example from the Brahms G major Sonata, the degree of curvature will be correspondingly  more acute. The movement also gives more freedom when playing on the E string. During an impassioned outburst, it lifts the arm from the side and gives an immediate sense of release. It should again be pointed out, however, that in the whole question of movement in the body, the aim is a sensitive interplay of stress and strain which should not be distractingly excessive: the needs of the music simply call for a natural response from the body.

A final aspect of the law of right-over-left is the position of the left elbow. The elbow should not lie comfortably at the side, but should be trained to move sufficiently under the instrument as to be seen there on its inner side by the player. Excess is not advocated. What is important is to see that this position helps to throw the body over to the left from the waist, and to raise the right arm from the side: it also allows the fingers to be raised high above the strings from which position they can 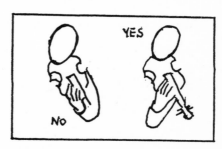 fall vertically and precisely like mechanical hammers. If there is resistance in the shoulder or a cramped feeling results, loosening exercises will be necessary and these should be done with reference to what has been said in the chapter on feeling awareness. The aim whilst playing is to achieve a pliable freedom at the shoulder— as though a cushion of air existed between the arm and the side, and although to this end we may have to stretch muscles, it can only be done on the basis of relaxation; nothing can be achieved with an attitude of aggression.

We come to an end of our study of right and left in relation to the mechanics of holding the violin. This has involved the angles at which the violin is held in relation to the bow, the general rule of weight on the left foot, a certain modification of this, and finally the rule of the left elbow. In the total picture, all combine in an easy and unaffected way to create the secure but flexible ground upon which further aspects of technique may be built.

4

BOW AND VIOLIN AS MALE AND FEMALE

THIS CHAPTER, though in a way a continuation of the right-left theme, now involves a consideration of the specific functions of the violin and the bow.

What is remarkable about the violin, and yet is so obvious that it is often overlooked, is that it is anthropomorphic both in the naming of its parts and in its shape. We have the names *back, belly, neck, ribs, breast-plate*, (and in the bow department even *heel*); and it requires no great stretch of imagination to see the essentially female form in the violin family, with its waistline and its solid foundation tapering in the upper half to gentler proportions. It may be objected that such a correspondence is accidental. But is any shape separable from its function? Are not all forms the outer expression of the purpose behind their existence? 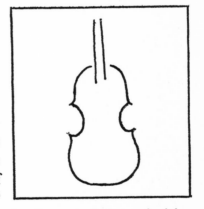 Seen in this light, the nose is a projection because it is a primitive seeker out of smell and the ear is a hollow burrowed out by sound. The shape of the cup and its function—to contain liquid —are one and the same, and the function of the chair is implicit in its form.

What then is the function embodied in the form of the violin: why has the form assumed female characteristics? It is clear that this form is not an ephemeral fashion, when we consider that during its whole history, it has undergone no radical change.

For hundreds of years violin makers, either consciously or unconsciously, have fashioned their instruments in this form, and it would seem that in relation to function, the point of greatest efficiency has been reached. No further improvement seems possible. What, however, is the actual function of the violin? To this question the truest answer would be—to give birth to sound. A violin is, after all, only an enclosed volume of air awaiting to be resonated by the bow for the purpose of producing sound. But to give birth is also the function of the female. She awaits impregnation by the male in order to beget other beings. It is here where we have to look for the correspondence between the violin and the female form: both are wombs of creation. There is even a parallel to be found in certain concepts of the creation of the world, where God is referred to as Father-Mother. The violin is like the 'Mother substantial' aspect, within which the bow, the 'Father initiative' aspect, acts to beget the world. In this sense, God himself can be seen as violin-bow.

Another significant aspect of the form of the violin is the tautened strings. Without tautness there can be no creation. Though the enclosed air is itself immobile and passive, there is at the same time, via the strings, a state of keyed-up anticipation. The strings, as it were, hold their formal possibilities in potential, hungering for the bow under the hand of the musician to awaken them to life.

The male principle obviously enough lies in the bow. The relationship between its form and its function need no further elucidation. It is the means of initiating the expenditure of energy and of creating life within the passive volume of air. The bow is significantly *bowed* or bent, thus giving tautness to the hair. The Greek word for bow is βιός (bios), and it is interesting to note that a related word βίος means life, indicating that the potential for life lies in the mobilisation of power within tension. The tautness of the hair is the male counterpart to the tautness of the strings, and the birth of sound is only possible through their mutual tension. In the act of playing, the tensions are, of course, different in character—whilst the bow evokes, the string responds. But the important thing is that they complement each other, and it is this that has to be remembered by the violinist. An over-aggressive bow can kill the potential for response from the instrument: on the other hand, an anaemic bow has no power to elicit any response at all from the instrument. Parallel situations of this kind can easily be found in human relationships.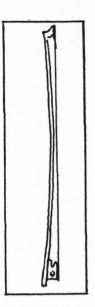

We have now seen the bow and violin as male and female (the technical aspect of this is discussed in the chapter *Co-ordination of bow and violin*), but the picture is incomplete without a third factor. We cannot speak of a creative process without considering the 'form' which is begotten of the father and the mother. In terms of the violin, this form is the notes which are articulated by the fingers of the left hand. These fingers, punctuating the open strings and shaping the sound by length and pitch, create their own universe of multifarious forms. The outpouring of sound which results from the playing of the violin is no imaginary creation. Sound *is* form—it is the ground of formal structure. This can be seen in the simplest of experiments done with fine sand on a drumskin, where, by resonating the skin at its different nodal points, geometric shapes are produced. Conversely, sound can be seen as destroyer where in more recent experiments it has been shown capable of disintegrating some of the hardest materials known to man. In whichever role, sound is the key to form. Violinists do not realise that they hold in their hands a potential miniature universe, and that when they play they set in motion the creative process and lay down their own universe of form. The unrolling of the destiny of this universe is symbolically represented by the scroll of the violin:

it is, as its shape suggests, the unfolding of the cosmic book of life.

What then is to be gained from this digression into realms apparently remote from the everyday instrument that lies in front of us? Firstly, it can draw attention to the fact of the two parts—violin and bow—each with its own specific function, and to the fact that wholeness can not be achieved until these parts work together in intimate relationship. Secondly, it is to emphasise that we cannot see the problems of playing in cold isolation —they are bound up with the mystery of life itself. If this is understood, all problems, including stance, relationship of right and left, co-ordination, right arm power, left hand precision, and many others, take on a much deeper significance.

5

HOLDING THE BOW

MANY DIFFICULTIES arise in the bowing arm because of an initial misconception about *holding* the bow. Nowhere is there a greater need for delicacy of touch and yet nowhere is more contraction found than in the right hand as it holds the bow. The first approach to the bow is usually, 'how can I hold it to keep it under control?' It should be 'how can I hold it with the least possible interference from the fingers and yet keep it in control?' This point of minimal interference is the key to the whole question: it is only when interference in excess of that point is eliminated that spontaneity is possible and the bow begins to play itself. A parallel could be drawn between the fingers on the bow and the relationship of a conductor with his orchestra. A conductor could profitably ask himself, 'how little can I do to allow my orchestra to play spontaneously and yet under the guidance of the music as I conceive it?'

This balance between spontaneity and control goes on through every facet of the performance of music, but so little is it considered in the initial stages of teaching that most young players can be seen 'controlling' the bow by excessive gripping from the fingers. The more they grip of course, the more they reduce efficiency. It is suggested therefore, to counter this danger, that the initial contact of the hand with the bow should be a passive rather than an active one. This can be achieved in the following way.

The hand is held in the position shown in the diagram—basically the playing position upturned. The bow, which has been lying with the nut projecting over the end of a table and

the hair uppermost parallel to it, is then taken by the hand from underneath: it now lies pivoted between the first finger and the thumb so that it has very little contact with the remaining fingers. Lying passively in the fingers in this way, there is no sense of the bow being controlled: it rests on the first finger, is balanced by the thumb, and feels almost to be without weight. The feeling of weightlessness in the bow can be emphasised even more by releasing it (throwing is too strong a term) upwards out of the fingers the smallest possible distance—say an eighth of an inch—and taking it on the return with the arm in movement as though catching a fast moving ball.

Once lightness of touch has been established in this passive position, the bow is then turned over with a slow twist of the forearm into what may be called an active position—that is, in readiness for playing near the heel. As it turns, the importance of the fourth finger taking the strain becomes apparent and the tendency of both the first and fourth fingers, and also the thumb, to control by gripping, can easily be seen. The first and fourth, also in order to control, tend to stretch out too far from the other fingers, causing tension in the back of the hand and the wrist. Both are major faults in holding the bow. The main object of the exercise is to be able to change from the passive to the active positions with the minimum of feeling change in the fingers: when the bow is held in perfect balance in the active position, so that the fingers merely restrain it from falling out of the hand, that can be called the point of minimal interference.

It is then helpful to apply this principle with the bow contacting the string. If the bow is allowed to rest on the string at varying points between heel and tip, the changing function of the fourth finger can readily be seen: and the effort to initiate a note in the upper half of the bow will indicate the importance of the first finger in that area. It is only when the problems of the source of power in the arm and the control of legato are studied that we really understand the advantage of such an early sensitising of the fingers, for we find then that another important principle has been allowed to operate freely. This briefly is that though the fingers are involved in varying ways according to the part of the bow being used, the type of bowing, and the dynamic required, at no time do they independently exert pressure: it is always some part of the arm that transmits what we have later termed weight through the fingers to the bow.

To sum up let us restate the important issue in this chapter. It is that control of the bow does not come of any form of gripping but paradoxically from a study of concepts like 'how little can the fingers do' and 'the point of minimal interference'. If this is understood and worked upon in the early years, the bow can later be handled with the sleight of hand of a conjurer.

6

THE LEFT HAND

THE DANGER of attempting to control by gripping threatens the left hand as well as the right. If the neck of the violin is held at all tightly, free movement is immediately inhibited. The hand, as part of the whole forearm unit moving up and down the fingerboard, should have the lightness and mobility of air; yet at the same time the fingers should work with the power and immediacy of mechanical hammers. Violinists who are aware of this, limber up before playing, establishing a free movement of the forearm from the elbow, and at the same time firing down the fingers so that their impact upon the string can be heard. The loose statement that the left hand holds the instrument needs careful re-appraisal. The hand does not in any way hold up or hold onto the instrument, and it should be able to release whatever tension has been involved, at any moment. Again, for maximum efficiency to be achieved it is a question of eliminating extraneous tensions. But before studying the physical issues in detail, it is proposed to take a closer look at the function of the fingers.

The fingers are, as we have said before, articulators of the structure of music. Their main function is to punctuate the open strings in order to create patterns of sound, and for this reason they must have, above all else, the quality of precision. As the word finger suggests—it has a close connection with the Latin *pingere*, to paint—the fingers are as the fingers of God that paint the separate structures in the universe. This is a cosmic defining process in which there is no overlapping: each form is different to the next. But mere defined form is not life and each form needs sustaining by a life giving energy. This energy is vibration. All in the universe vibrates at its own particular frequency which constitutes its emotive life. (This is discussed in greater detail in the chapter on vibrato.) Consequently for the violinist, the fingers have a dual function. Although they define notes precisely, they also have the added task of charging the defined notes with feeling. The rhythmic pulsing that does this is known as vibrato.

It should be said here of vibrato, however, that although it is expressed through the fingers, it does not originate in them. Feeling, as we will see later, is essentially a function of the fore-arm. Also the danger in the term *precision* should be seen clearly. Though the root of precision, the Latin *praecisionem*, implies a cutting off and a separating of notes from each other, at the same time, as in a universe where all beings are interdependent and interpenetrative, no note stands in isolation. It and its feeling life are involved in relationship with a preceding note, a sub-sequent note, and a whole pattern of notes.

For the moment it is intended to consider ways in which the primary function of articulation can best be developed. They will be set down as a series of eight considerations.

Consideration 1: The pre-condition of articulation by the fingers is that the elbow is held well under the violin in order that the fingers may be raised into a position of command above the strings.

Consideration 2: The root of finger power is at the base of the knuckles, and power should be felt to derive from that place. This means that the fingers must be clear of and above 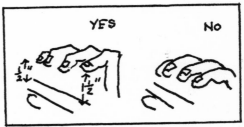 the line of the fingerboard. They can then be pulled back into a position, alert and constantly ready for attack, like snakes poised for the kill. No power can come from fingers that resemble dying tulips. In action their movement should be that of mechanical hammers firing down and returning to an original point of balance.

Consideration 3: The point to which the fingers return above the strings is important. Firstly, it is here where the fingers mobilise themselves for action. This means that there should be the least possible degree of tension at this point, or their attacking power is impaired. In slow motion, an individual finger should fire down onto the string at high speed, make firm but brief and elastic contact, release tension, and finally find itself lightly poised for action in the initial position. (For a more complete study of an attack the reader is referred to the chapter on *Some Aspects of Power* where an attack by the bow arm is analysed: the laws are identical for either finger or arm).

Secondly, the point of return should be constant and the fingers, either individually or as a group, should return to it automatically when not playing. Undisciplined movement of the fingers only impairs their precision and power. Due to the lie of the hand, the height of the fingers above the strings varies —say between a half an inch and an inch and a half, the greater height helping the naturally weaker third and fourth fingers. But this should not preclude them remaining close together and working as a compact unit. (See diagram, page 43.)

Consideration 4: The wrist should never break the line that extends from the elbow to the knuckles. If it bends and the neck of the violin sits in the palm of the hand, however slightly,

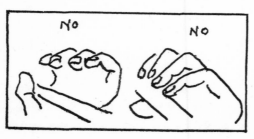

tension is produced in the wrist and the vertical fall of the fingers is impeded. If the wrist bends in the other direction, the fingers are unable to command the lower strings, and again the vertical fall is impeded and tension is caused in both wrist and fingers. The forearm from the elbow to the knuckles should always be felt as an unbroken unit as it moves up and down the fingerboard.

Consideration 5: The line of the finger-tips above the strings, and thus of the hand itself, should be as near parallel to the line of the strings as possible. This is not practicable unless the elbow is well under the violin: nor is it practicable if the thumb and the root of the first finger lock on the neck of the violin as the fingers move over from the lower to the upper strings. To counter 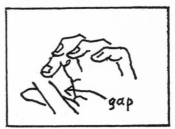 this tendency, the hand should be trained to move out gently from the neck, using the thumb as a pivot. In this way, particularly when playing on the A and E strings, a slight gap is created between the hand and the fingerboard which removes all possibility of locking.

Consideration 6: In no sense does the thumb hold the instrument. Its function is to balance the downwards pressure of the fingers as they drive into the string: an attempt to use the fingers without the thumb readily clarifies this point. The 'pressure balance' between fingers and thumb is so sensitive as to allow the hand to be taken away from the neck at a moment's notice. On the G string it should project very little above the fingerboard (though this is modifiable according to the length of the thumb), and for the other strings should move progressively under the neck of the violin, allowing the gap referred to in Consideration 5.

Consideration 7: Because it is not used so vigorously as the right arm, the left arm is often ignored and tends to become rigid. Such rigidity can only hinder finger dexterity. The shoulder and elbow should be simultaneously flexible whilst playing and the following exercise is suggested to this end. The violin should be held firmly under the chin and the whole forearm unit moved lightly towards and away from the body alongside the finger-board. As it does so the fingers should be made to rise and fall as though playing: this gives a simultaneous flexing of the elbow and the knuckles. Then the whole arm should be made to move across from the shoulder in front of the body and back again with the fingers rising and falling in the same way: this gives a simultaneous flexing of the shoulder and the knuckles. Similar exercises without the instrument should in fact be done before the acquisition of a left hand technique, and should certainly accompany its development. A useful device to give buoyancy in the arm whilst playing is the same as that for giving freedom at the shoulder: a mental picture of a cushion of air between the arm and the side.

Consideration 8: Vibrato should not interfere with the precision of the fingers. In the early stages much confusion is caused by the introduction of vibrato before precision has been mastered. It then becomes merely a camouflage for inaccuracy.

7

CO-ORDINATION OF BOW AND VIOLIN

ONE OF THE most common weaknesses of style is the lack of a
sense of unity between the bow and the violin. Although the bow
itself may seem alive enough, the total impression is of it acting
upon a dead instrument: there is an unhappy feeling of two
parts working separately from each other rather than working
in harmonious relationship. This relationship of bow and violin
we have already likened to that of male and female in which
male evokes and female responds. These images help in the
understanding of the act of playing because though different in
character, together they make a unity—a unity that should be
felt by the violinist as his bow moves over the string and especially when it re-establishes contact with the string after a rest. It
is to this end that the following exercises are suggested.

In the first, there is no contact between bow and violin. Both
arms should be mobile and airborne in feeling, and the bow held
at its mid-point, approximately a third of an inch above the
string. Bow and violin are then made to move, as though joined
by an invisible thread, in all directions—sideways, upwards,
downwards and in circles—until there is no tendency for them
to separate. If this is done regularly, the feeling is soon acquired
of two halves that have merged into a co-ordinated whole.

In the second, a short up bow at the tip takes the bow in a
gentle arc to the heel. Here it remains, as before, poised about a
third of an inch above the string—still without touching it. Now,
the object is to sense the unity of the bow and the violin by a
delicate movement in both arms like that of the wings of a seagull
hovering on a thermal. This effortless fluctuation continues for

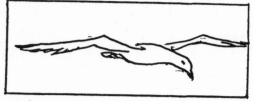

some time, until the bow is allowed to alight gently on the string. The same can now be repeated starting with a down bow so that the bow is poised at the tip.

This exercise can be varied by eliminating the poise above the string and allowing the bow to land immediately. As it does so,

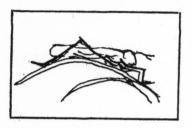

there is a yield from the instrument, as sensitive, to draw on nature again, as a blade of grass bending under an alighting grasshopper.

This is the fine degree of control a player should aim for: pin-point contact, which comes from the feeling of unity between bow and string, is essential if his playing is to be sensitive. Beginnings of individual notes and phrases, no matter how gentle or violent, depend upon unity in the poise which immediately precedes action. And in the course of playing, there is a giving and a receiving from both sides reminiscent of the perfect understanding of the rider and his horse.

8

THE RIGHT ARM

THE FUNCTION of the right arm is diametrically opposed to that of the left hand. As we have already seen in the chapter on right and left, the right side represents will or free energy, as opposed to reason or enclosed energy. It is here in the right arm that a man's executive power lies: the universal energy in him works through it to create or to destroy. He wills to 'do' and the arm carries out the intention of the will.

The essential aim of this energy, seen most clearly in the animal world, where it is least inhibited, is the immediate achievement of a desired objective. The appetites of an animal are not subject to consideration: will is without meditation and entirely spontaneous. In man, this spontaneity has a correspondence in the structure of the body—the arm at the shoulder from where action stems, has assumed the form of a ball and socket which allows relatively uninhibited movement. But despite nature's help, man's complexity—his fears and his intellectual taboos on raw energy—has contributed to creating blockages in his physical body and in destroying his animal freedom. For any physical activity, whether it be boxing, tennis, fencing or playing the violin, this freedom has to be refound or the energy potential within him will remain unrealised.

It is for this reason that the following exercises are suggested. They must always be done with reference to what has been said in the chapter on feeling awareness, for movement as such is valueless. The aim of the exercises themselves is the freeing of places that are habitually blocked, not only at the shoulder but also at all other joints, so that ultimately the arm may become completely flexible and able to act at lightning speed. All except movement 1 are related to particular aspects of playing. It is suggested that they are done initially without the bow so that there is no interference from the concept of *holding* the bow. When violin and bow are held the exercises may be repeated, bearing in mind the relationship of each movement to its role whilst playing.

Movement 1: This is a piston movement in which the arm is kept close to the side and the forearm parallel to the ground.

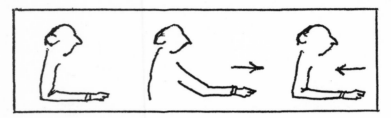

Movement 2: This movement is similar to No. 1 but with the whole arm raised from the side and kept parallel to the ground

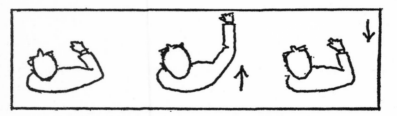

in approximately playing position. It corresponds in playing to the placing of the bow at a given point between the fingerboard and the bridge. Control of this point is the basis of both tone quality and dynamics.

Movement 3: The arm, from a raised position parallel to the ground is alternately lowered and raised from the side without the forearm moving out of plane with the upper arm. The movement, which depends upon flexibility at the shoulder, is the basis of all crossing of the strings and should be absolutely smooth and machine-like in its working.

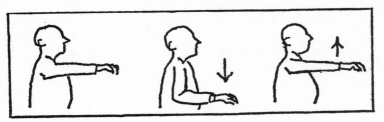

Movement 4: The raised arm of No. 3 is raised a little higher than it naturally wishes to go. This upwards stretch is invaluable

in various ways; for instance, in lifted staccato, when the arm is poised for an attack, or for any movement of the bow through the air.

Movement 5: The hand draws imaginary wide circles, clockwise and anti-clockwise, in front of the head These circles are in

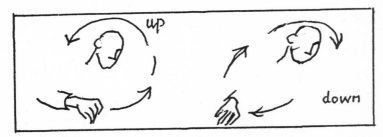

effect continuations of up bows and down bows, and are intended to develop the follow-through at the end of a bow stroke. Too often a down bow comes to a sticky end by the side and an up bow stops prematurely before the heel is reached.

Movement 6: The arm, in a position for playing at the heel, is forced to the left in front of the face. This stretching operation

has something of the same purpose as No. 5. Its aim is to release the unused last nine inches of bow so that they are played with the same facility as the upper half.

Movements 7 and 8: These two simple movements from the elbow can be grouped together. No. 7 is a simple right to left movement of the forearm and No. 8 is as near a rotation of the forearm as it is possible to achieve from the elbow. Both are designed to increase flexibility at the elbow as is required in détaché and legato.

Movement 9: This is a simple rotation of the hand from the wrist. Power in the bow arm depends a great deal upon there being no contraction in the wrist.

Movement 10: Here the fingers contract and stretch, working independently of the hand from the knuckles. The hand is held with the thumb touching the tips of the first and second fingers, as though the bow were being held. The fingers are first drawn up and then pushed out converging to a point, the whole alternating process resembling the legs of the swimmer in action.

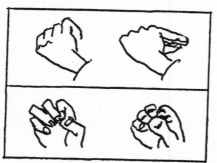

Finger flexibility is of the utmost importance when playing near the heel, when changing bow and for certain types of staccato.

Once all these movements have been mastered and there remains no unnecessary resistance in the muscles, the bow may then, and only then, be used with the agility, the sensitivity and the ferocity of an animal. More of this relationship with the animal kingdom will be discussed in the next chapter which concerns various aspects of power.

9

SOME ASPECTS OF POWER

Its source in the right arm

We have defined the function of the right arm and suggested exercises to achieve flexibility in it. But what, now, is the nature of the power applied through the arm that realises the maximum sound potential of an instrument. To use the term *pressure* would be misleading since it has overtones of a hard squeezing force that would be a limitation on power. And yet some form of downwards force is applied. This force can be more accurately described as *weight* because weight is free of associations with contraction. An arm can weigh down without inner muscular contraction. The degree of weight, then, determines the degree of power produced—but only partially.

Weight itself is inert, and for energy to be imparted to a string, another factor is involved. This factor is movement: and the more movement there is the greater is the degree of energy imparted. This principle can clearly be seen in everyday occurrences—the faster the blow from the fist, for example, the more likely it is to knock a person down. (It is more obvious that the heavier the fist, the greater will be the power behind the blow.) Many instrumentalists do not realise that speed as well as weight in the bow increases the amplitude of the vibration of a string, and that dynamics are regulated by an interplay between the two. When a level dynamic is required throughout the whole of a phrase, as in this example from the Sibelius Concerto, a continual adjustment is taking place -at one point weight making up for slower movement, and at another, greater speed making up for less weight. (Notably the C♯ in the second com-

plete bar and the G and the A crotchets in the fourth bar.)
Such a situation can be found in practically every line of music.

Power is restricted, however, because both weight and speed
are impeded by tensions in the physical body. As far as weight is
concerned, the severest limitation comes of general contraction
in the arm and especially in the fingers. If the fingers are
tightened upon the bow in an exaggerated manner, it can easily
be felt how potential weight is taken back into the contracted
fingers and the hair of the bow skates weakly over the surface
of the string. In the correct application of weight, the fingers,
especially the first finger, lean on the bow, only transmitting
weight supplied by the different parts of the arm. Weight is also
impeded when the elbow
is raised too high or when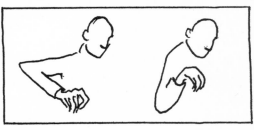
it is too close to the side.
In both cases the plane of
the arm is destroyed, the
wrist is forced into a
cramped position and the
bow becomes dependent upon pressure from the fingers. The most
helpful guiding concept could be said to be that of the arm weigh-
ing downwards in one plane from the base of the knuckles to
shoulder. But though this applies perfectly to the middle of the
bow, it is not consistent near the heel where the elbow needs to
be lowered producing a consequent upwards bend at the wrist,
nor at the tip where there is a tendency for a slight downwards
bend at the wrist. We have in fact to sub-divide the arm and
modify that plane since it is clear that, in the lower half of the
bow, weight comes from the upper arm, that after the middle it

comes from the forearm, and that at the tip it comes from the hand itself. The problem is obviously one of maintaining consistency through these transitions: and how can this be possible without complete manœuvrability at the shoulder, the elbow, the wrist and within the fingers through which the weight operates. The same problem will appear again when legato bowing is considered. (On the E string, where the overall weight of the arm is not felt so naturally, it is a help to refer to the body movement described on page 32.)

As far as speed is concerned, it too is hindered by contraction in the arm. This can be seen most clearly near the heel of the bow when a locked shoulder slows down the movement of the arm. Equally, speed is hindered by anticipation of the bow change, where an appreciable slowing down can often be heard. As a remedy for this, the bow should be imagined to be six inches longer than it really is and should aim beyond its destination as a sprinter aims at a point beyond the finishing line so as not to lose momentum. The speed of the bow must be maintained through its whole length so that the change of direction takes place at the last second.

Animal attack

When the bow begins a note with force from a state of rest, it can be said to have made an attack. But it does not arbitrarily hit the string—there are certain conditions to be met before an attack can achieve maximum power. The foremost of these is that it should be initiated from a state of minimal tension. This is to say, that prior to the attack there should be only that degree of tension in the arm sufficient to retain it in an extended position. This state has already been seen in our study of feeling awareness, and elsewhere: it so little resembles tension in feeling that it has been described as light, free, and weightless. These words are of course inaccurate, because the weight of the arm is itself a force of inertia that has to be overcome, and they should therefore be read with this qualification—that all that can be achieved in the physical body is a minimal tension.

The whole question is best studied in the animal kingdom. When the cat lies drowsily on the grass or the lizard is still in the sand, its energy is not drawn in to a centre: it is, as it were, spread out. Its bio-field—that field of energy surrounding and permeating any living organism—is in its most relaxed state. But when the lizard has seen the fly or the cat the bird, there is a sudden transformation: there is now an intent to action—an in-drawing and an in-holding of that field of energy. The bio-field is now toned up and mobilised for action. In this new state however, the important thing to notice is that there is still no muscular tension, with the result that the tongue or the paw,

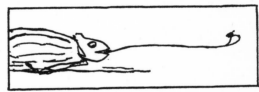

when it moves into action, does so at lightning speed. A violinist, when he has indrawn energy for an attack, must take care that his physical body is still at the minimal tension level, or his power will be impeded. If he follows correctly a three-fold process of—minimal tension, intent to action, and attack, he can pounce on the string with the immediacy of the animal.

What is so amazing about an attack in the animal world, is how it seems to be deferred until the last possible moment. There is, as it were, a super-charged stillness. If a parallel is to be found for the violinist, it would be the stillness of the bow on the string immediately before the attack. This is another condition then, of a powerful attack. The bow must descend vertically onto the string and remain there with a momentary stillness before the note is played. Without this, precision is lost and the bite of the bow on the string is neither felt nor heard.

For the sake of clarity, it is suggested that an attack on a single sforzando note should be analysed in slow motion as follows.

Stage I: Bow held with minimal tension half an inch above the string.

Stage II: Bow in same position—energy now indrawn—bow poised for attack.

Stage III: The attack (a) vertical descent of bow on string —still and weightless.

(b) an immediate free release of energy.

Stage IV: Return after note is played to original minimal tension state.

It is true that at speed, such stages will not be felt individually, but as in all technical matters, it is accuracy in slow motion that lays the foundation for efficiency at speed.

Our concept of the term attack also has to be a wide one. Whether violent, as on the E♯ in this example from the Sibelius

Concerto, or more gentle, as on the high D in the next example from Mozart's A major Concerto, the process is the same. It is essential that immediately before these notes the bow arm itself should be weightless, and that there should be a still and

weightless contact of the bow on the string. The image of the lizard should not deceive us by its delicacy. The shooting out of its tongue to catch the fly is equally an attack, and for it, constitutes power. This power of the lizard can be emulated by playing short delicate notes, taking the bow from tip to heel and heel to tip through the air

at speed, whilst still observing the four stages described.

This analysis of power as attack may be considered unnecessarily complex, but it is only through such an approach that arbitrariness can be reduced and immediacy achieved. Instrumentalists, as well as athletes, would do well to study the animal kingdom. The electric vitality to be found there is what keeps the attention of an audience riveted to a performance.

The subtle source of power

We have seen that the right arm gives expression to a universal energy which can either create or destroy, and we have studied the mobilisation of that energy for an attack through the arm. But the arm itself cannot be said to be the source of that energy. The legs as they walk, sexual power, the drive needed to accomplish an arduous feat, or the violence of the killer all avail themselves of the same source of energy.

To understand this, it is necessary to refer to the fundamental division of the human organism into head, chest, and abdomen. Each of these physical areas has a subtle counterpart, so that broadly speaking, thinking can be said to be located in the head, feeling can be said to have its seat in the chest area, and action can be said to stem from the sub-diaphragmatic area. Such knowledge of the body and its inner sources of power are known and used by all esoteric religions and systems of self-realisation.

Of the different types of energy lying below the diaphragm we cannot be concerned here. The focal point of pure animal drive, however, lies more specifically in an area just below the navel, and it is this that should be brought into consciousness. Exercises of the feeling awareness variety may be used to do this, but the most effective way is through the use of low diaphragmatic breathing. Such breathing gives a downwards movement of consciousness which culminates in the navel area. The result is a sense of being firmly rooted to the ground and also a capacity for high speed motor response in the limbs, in which the requirements of a given situation and the response to it in action, become virtually simultaneous. In such simultaneity, there is no room for interference from the mind, which, by comparison, is laboriously slow. The classical example of this type of energy usage is the Zen warrior whose stance disguises an explosive energy that can be mobilised at lightning speed.

The ability to draw on this source of energy is invaluable to the violinist, who, as a Westerner, is in danger of a disbalance in favour of the head. To be able to incorporate it in the act of playing guards against the danger of a brilliant technique not being sufficiently vitalised: a technique is essential, but only insofar as it dispenses with notes and mechanics and allows an uninterrupted flow of power.

Power in circulation

The universe can be viewed as a field of energy which has concentrated itself at certain focal points where it rotates. An energy system can be small, as an atom, or vast, as a galaxy: both have the common property of rotation. Rotation, is in fact, synonymous with natural order: it is not necessary to quote the many instances in everyday life where smoothness and efficiency of functioning depend upon free circulation. Moreover, the circle, which turns back upon itself and is without end, symbolises the infinite and eternity, whereas the line with its end and its beginning symbolises the finite and time.

Which quality are we to incorporate into our playing—the smoothness and endlessness of the circle or the angularity and finiteness of the line? It is surprising how much this concept of a circle can infect and liberate the quality of playing in a stringed instrument. The simple exercise illustrated in the diagram, aims

at this sense of liberation at the end of a bow stroke. An up bow, starting at the tip is made to follow through in front of the face. It performs a wide circle and returns delicately to the point from which it sets out. By comparison, if at the end of the up bow the arm is drawn back in a linear manner, and only the actual length of the bow is used, the feeling given is of restriction and abruptness. The original exercise can be repeated using a down bow, and varied by playing longer or shorter notes at different tempos. In the illustration, for instance, taking the tempo ♪=60, the circle need only cover say a quarter of the

bow length: or supposing the notes to be demi-semiquavers and the tempo to be doubled, only one inch of bow needs to be used. At whatever speed, the aim is for the bow to describe a circular movement through the air, alighting precisely and delicately at the point of departure.

It is true that little will be seen of this circle at high speed, but benefit will always be felt from having studied it in slow motion. Its value can be seen in almost any page of music. In this

example from the Beethoven Quartet Op. 18 No. 1, the circular movement following through from the D crotchet allows a sensitive return to the tip, poising the bow in readiness for the B demi-semiquaver. Or in the slow movement of the Schubert Sonatina in D, the recovery of the bow between the third and

fourth bars is accomplished more efficiently by a graceful arc through the air. The circle is invaluable to the string player: it can give a sense of flow from note to note, liberate a heavy style of playing, and introduce hope into an orchestral player's arm halfway through the third Messiah of a season.

Power in the vibrated string

The last aspect of power to be considered is to do with the behaviour of a resonated string in relation to the bow which resonates it. Although this subject can be found in most music courses under the heading of acoustics, its practical application to string playing is severely neglected.

The most important property of a resonated string is that its power potential varies according to the point at which it is bowed. If a string is bowed at its mid-point, only a muffled noise will be heard—the vibration of the string has been impeded at the point of its greatest amplitude. This demonstrates the law *ad absurdum.* But on the same principle there is an enormous difference in the sound of a string bowed just over the finger-board, and one bowed

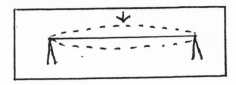

two inches higher near the bridge. The actual mechanics of this can easily be observed. When, say, the D string is bowed near the bridge, the amplitude of the vibration is so great as to nearly touch the G and A strings on either side. When played near the fingerboard, scarcely any vibration can be seen at all. The difference in the actual sound is enormous. Each dynamic seeks its own appropriate place, and it is clearly as illogical for a *forte* to be played near the fingerboard as it is for a *piano* to be played near the bridge.

At the same time, the point at which the string is bowed also affects the quality of the sound. A pianissimo over the finger-board giving a flautando sound, is not the same pianissimo that can be achieved by playing with a lighter bow near the bridge. Similarly, a forte played very near the bridge will produce a very different sound to one played at the mid-point between fingerboard and bridge: such effects are common property to all instrumentalists.

These are simple properties of a resonated string and yet despite this, the placing of the bow is frequently ignored, with the all too common sight of players moving the bow in a restricted area over and near the fingerboard. It should be possible to place the bow at any point between the bridge and the finger-board and to keep it undeviatingly at that point during a passage which involves frequent crossing of the strings. Only when a player can do this will he be able to control dynamic and tone quality.

Power in a resonated string is also greatly dependent upon the angle made by the bow to the string. For the maximum potential to be realised, the bow should move at an angle of 90° to the

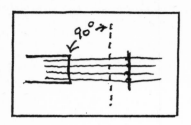

string, that is in a line parallel with the bridge. The greater the deviation from the right angle, the more the bow interferes with the free flow of vibration, loses grip, and causes impure tone production. An incorrectly angled bow is one of the chief causes of a fluctuating tone and loss of power, which can easily be appreciated by varying the angle of the bow in an exaggerated manner during a sustained note.

Another aspect of the science of the vibrated string is the angle

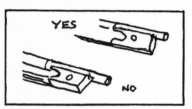

made by the hair of the bow as it contacts the string. With the bow held correctly, the problem does not arise, but if the wrist bends, tilting the bow too far over, only the edge of the hair is able to contact the string, and an anaemic tone results. On the other hand, if the hair is flat, it is spread over too wide a surface and interferes with the vibrations. The hair produces most power when slightly angled from the vertical as in the diagram: in this position it is so compacted as to give a firm decisive contact with the string. For evenness of tone to be sustained, the angle of the hair should not be varied throughout the length of the bow.

Also in the bow/string relationship, there is the more obvious effect of the degree of tension in bow-hair itself. Bow-hair which is slack has too great an area of contact with the surface of the string and interferes with the vibrations: bow-hair which is tight has too little an area of contact so that it is unable to get a hold of the string to vibrate it. The mean tension at which the string responds freely and which is relative to the qualities of the particular bow (and of course to the amount of resin—without resin there is no friction whatever), can only be discovered by personal experiment.

Having considered these aspects of the bow/string relationship, it is useful to have an image of one ingredient which is common to all. This can best be described as a sense of frictional contact, for the bow only produces sound from the string by overcoming its resistance. In slow motion, the string is seen to be pulled in the direction of the movement of the bow until at a certain point its tension overcomes the pull and it springs back to its original position: the process then repeats itself. This is the essential nature of the contact between bow and string. It is a definite friction which must be felt by the violinist as he plays and which is the basis of a firm and resonant tone.

We have now looked at power from various aspects. Ideally all these aspects work together towards realising the maximum potential of the instrument. The movement that results will have that quality of beauty which is the hall-mark of all efficiency. Efficient power, whether it be in the wheel of the steam engine, the leap of the cat onto a high wall, or the arm of a violinist, is always beautiful, seeming to be simple and effortless in its working. In our study of legato that follows, this should be remembered: efficiency and grace of movement are here very closely related.

CONTROL IN LEGATO

The parallel bow

As we have seen under the heading of *Power in the vibrated string*, purity of tone depends upon the bow moving consistently in a line parallel to the bridge. The natural bow stroke of the beginner is a curved sweep around from one side of the body to the

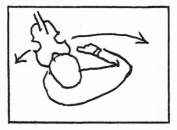

other—the arm has not yet divided itself into flexible parts and wants to move in one unit from the shoulder. This simple issue remains the major problem of violinists. How can the curve be avoided and a line be carried through from the extreme tip to the extreme heel of the bow? There are three factors involved in this.

Firstly, there is the tendency in the up bow for the upper arm to lock near the heel. This causes the wrist to be used in compensation, and a curve is made to complete the bow stroke. To remedy this, tensions at the shoulder must be freed, so that as the heel is approached the arm can be brought easily in towards the body. The parallel line can then be maintained, and the change of bow effected by the wrist and fingers with the slightest of movements.

Secondly, in the down bow, there is a reluctance on the part of the forearm to move independently of the upper arm, and, as the tip is approached, for more locking at the shoulder to take place. Again, in compensation, the bow is forced into a curve.

The remedy, as before, is flexibility at the elbow and the shoulder, allowing free adjustment of the line.

Thirdly, there is the factor of flexible fingers. If the fingers are rigid and grip the bow, contraction spreads through the arm, and this again causes the curve in the bow stroke. They must be flexible enough to allow the bow to be constantly readjusted within them so that their respective balancing functions may operate freely. It should also be remembered again that the fingers are basically transmitters of weight—they do not independently exert pressure.

Though much work may be done, the tendency to lose line at the ends of the bow remains very strong. It is strong enough to

justify the exercise illustrated in the diagram, in which sustained bow strokes are made to veer slightly outwards in a direction contrary to the natural curve. The corrective effect of this exercise, once it is forgotten in the process of playing, is quite considerable.

The 'break' in the bow

The 'break' in the bow is tied up with the issues of the parallel line just discussed, and also with the whole question of leverage in the bow arm and the fingers. In order to maintain a uniform dynamic through the length of the bow, a complex play between the weight applied by the arm and the varying functions of the fingers is required. (It is not proposed to describe these processes in great detail: the printed word has a limit of usefulness, and the co-ordination of what has been already described under the headings of *Some Aspects of Power* and *Holding the Bow* is best studied by experiment.) But one thing that stands out above all others is the crucial moment, called the 'break' in the bow, when the upper arm hands over responsibility to the forearm. This handing over of responsibility is of the same kind that passes between two runners in a relay race—the function of one has to merge into the function of the other to give an imperceptible translation. Not only must the bow continue in a straight line but it must be able to continue with a uniform weight and at a uniform speed, and this can only be achieved if there is constant attention to flexibility within the elbow.

It is interesting that the difficulty arises at the transition from the power function of the upper arm to the naturally less stable feeling function of the forearm—but more is said of the different parts of the arm in the chapter on vibrato. If the mechanics of the parallel bow and leverage have been studied, there is normally no problem, but under conditions of 'concert nerves' and at a pianissimo dynamic, interference quickly shows at this vulnerable point of change. In these conditions players are left to find their own counter measures which may be against all laws of technique. The problem is so universal that violinists would do well to forgive themselves and others from the beginning. In the orchestral world, the conductor could help by remembering that the demand to produce less sound when the limit has already been reached, can only aggravate this problem and cause the arm to seize up altogether: thus he should allow as much movement as possible without destroying the tone quality he seeks.

Evenness of tone
Another vital factor in the control of legato is the maintaining of uniformity in the speed of the bow. It has already been seen that an increased speed increases the dynamic, yet it is not sufficiently realised that the smallest fluctuations in speed affect evenness of tone. Such fluctuations can occur anywhere in the bow, but it is at the ends where we find the most error. The last notes of a slurred group are often considerably weaker than the first

because the bow has initially travelled too fast and has then had to reduce speed. The bow, in other words has not been scientific-ally divided according to note values.

In the opening of the Mozart A major Concerto, for instance,

the usual enthusiastic burst can be heard on the dotted crotchets, at the expense of the weaker sounding quavers. The answer—of primary school simplicity—is to divide the bow into four quarters: three for the dotted crotchet and one for the quaver. Similarly in the opening of the Mendelssohn Concerto, the

minim B and its equivalent E in the next bar usually arrive precipitously at the tip, thus depriving of strength the crotchets that follow in the same bow. In this instance, of course, the bow should be divided into three.

Because it is a fundamental issue, to be found in any line of music, strict division of the bow should be practised right from the beginning of training until it becomes second nature. Rhythmic complexity is often found to confuse bow control and cause unevenness in speed and consequent fluctuation of tone. The following simple exercises should not be scorned. Notes should be played in slow motion and with mathematical exactness. Each bar can be taken individually and repeated, or taken as part of the whole group. In either case, first a whole bow should be used, and then a half a bow, until fine control of

speed is acquired. If this control has not been mastered in the early days, co-ordination may remain a permanent impasse and the bow may find itself in difficulties every time it meets with a complex rhythm in the fingers. Should this be the case, the method of separating the two parts is a great help. A passage is taken—preferably one bow stroke at a time, and the notes are omitted so that only the open string is played in the time of the passage: three things are watched carefully—the exact amount of bow to be used, the exact time of its duration and the evenness of its speed. Once this has been established, the rhythm or melody is then imaged mentally with it. Even to do this is likely to bring about disturbance in the bow: but the stage must be mastered—the power of mental imagery can not be stressed enough. At the final stage when the fingers themselves are superimposed, it will be found that the mental image has prepared the way for co-ordination and that the bow has achieved a sense of independence and an evenness of flow.

Finally we turn to the ends of the bow again: there is still the problem of maintaining evenness of tone at the very moment of the bow change. To succeed in this the wrist and fingers are best thought of as carrying through a momentum that has already been established by the whole arm. If this, and the image suggested elsewhere of aiming past a finishing line, are kept in mind, the change can be made without interruption and at the last possible moment.

II

APPLICATION AND RELEASE OF ENERGY
Certain Types of Staccato

THE PRINCIPLE of the application and release of energy has already been seen under the guise of power as attack. In the image of the cat, we saw how the pounce on the bird can be initiated at lightning speed because during the time the energy is mobilised for action, there is no contraction in the limbs. This state in the arm of the violinist, which has been variously referred to as a state of minimal tension, freedom, or weightlessness, is the source of his bow control. Unless he is able to return to it and attack from it at will, his playing will lack the immediacy of the animal. All music is a continual alternation between energy applied and energy released—between, in fact, notes and rests—and unless during the rests there is the greatest possible muscular relaxation in the arm, the notes will not be played efficiently. Expressed in mechanical terms—if a muscle is in a state of continual tension, it becomes insensitive to nervous impulses and is unable to respond adequately.

Perhaps the greatest benefit of the return to maximum relaxation in the arm, is the fine control possible over the rest itself. In this passage from the Mozart B♭ Sonata, recovering

the bow after the two semiquaver rests in time to give precisely articulated entries, is entirely dependent upon a momentary relaxation of tension. The stillness of the bow on the string before such entries, which has elsewhere been described as super-charged, can only be so called when the rests have been given their fullest value. So much of what is known as vitality comes from the suspense of delaying a rest until the last moment. In the example from the Mozart D major Concerto, there is no

actual written rest in which to prepare a precise F♯ entry following the sustained dotted crotchet on the A string. But a rest is implicit in the phrasing, and this depends upon the ability of the arm to take the bow across the string weightlessly and at high speed.

In the orchestral world, the rest is everything. Conductors are justified in shaking a head when players come in fractionally too soon. Rhythmic tension can only be maintained by regarding rests as sustained silences—not as gaps between notes. In this example from the *Eine kleine Nachtmusik*, this tension comes of

the suspense created by delaying the rest until the last microsecond. Such rests, written or unwritten, abound in every line of music, and in them, whether the bow remains on or is taken off the string, the bow arm must return to a state as free and mobile as air.

The rest can also be referred to in another way as *the virtue of space*. Space underlies all apparent solidity. The electro-microscope reveals that all so-called matter is energy in rotation: in the atom for instance, certain definable entities rotate in space much greater than themselves. In a larger common such as the solar system, only the minutest part is so-called dense matter. When human beings cry out for space, as from a confined city, or in a relationship which has become close to the point of mutual destruction, space *to be oneself* is the only remedy. Or space can be regarded on a more subtle level, as when a man is so identified with a situation that he has no space within him from which to look objectively at the situation and himself. This is the space needed by the confined spirit and lies at the very root of self awareness. For the musician, space has the same function; it allows notes to *be*. Manipulation of space is a performer's foremost weapon. As an actor's most powerful lines are his silences, so a musician's most telling moments are his rests.

The principle of application and release of energy lies behind much bowing technique. Especially in détaché, martelé, or slurred staccato, special attention should be paid to the tension

state in the arm. The example, from the Beethoven Romance in F, should be practised in slow motion with exaggerated gaps between the notes, in which the bow is lifted from the string and replaced with the delicacy of a thistledown.

The principle still applies in lifted staccato but the mechanics are now more complex. Once lifted off the string, the bow must return to it for the next note. If the bow makes that return whilst in horizontal movement, the beginning of the note loses definition. Before the articulation of each note therefore, the bow must alight vertically upon the string. Thus we have a four-fold process; a lift, a vertical descent, a weightless contact with the string, and a bite on the string. The beginning of the Bach Gavotte in E major can be condensed diagrammatically, as  shown, and should be practiced with this four-fold process in mind. If, for purposes of demonstration, the bowing were changed to two ups and a down, the same vertical descent of the bow on the string would apply; and at a faster speed, this familiar rhythm would benefit from slow motion analysis having been done.

There is, naturally, a point at which speed wins, but it is surprising in such passages how long the vertical bite of the bow into the string remains effective. It is not intended here, how-ever, to study the refinements of all types of bowing between a controlled staccato and a spontaneous bounce. Permutations of speed, dynamic, placing in the bow, and tone quality required, are ill-suited to verbal description and are best left to personal teaching and experiment.

In this chapter entitled *Application and Release of Energy*, it may be thought that little time has been devoted to application. Rhythmic tension, it is true, is equally dependent upon the correct observation of note values, and sometimes the effectiveness of a rest depends upon the slight shortening of the time value of a note. The aim has been more to emphasise the relationship of the rest with the tension state of the arm, and to affirm that there is a technique of playing rests, which, once it has been considered a worthy object of study, will enable a player to hold an audience on the edge of their seats.

This subject cannot be left without reference to the role of the index finger. The index finger leans on the bow at the first joint and can be seen as an extension of the arm, affirming the energy being expended through it. (For this affirming role observe the beginning of each note of the example from the Beethoven Romance (page 73) taken in slow motion.) But its role is a dual one, for it also releases and sensitises that energy at will, controlling weight moment by moment at any point of the bow. Thus, in this question of application and release we have to be conscious of both the arm and the index finger. The index finger, restraining and controlling, can be seen in life where it points the way in which our energies are going to be used or when it wags in moral condemnation. It is essentially an instrument of intellectual control and is very important to the violinist. The control is operative at all times—in sustained bowing where in order to maintain a uniform dynamic the function of the finger changes as the bow moves from tip to heel, or in an immediate attack and release as in up bow slurred staccato. (Take the notes of the Beethoven example with this type of bowing at varying speeds.) But the whole time it is ready for one thing or another, for affirming or controlling, applying or releasing energy expended by the arm. As a knife being used with the blade towards the body must be pressed and yet for safety withheld, so must these opposites be contained in the index finger in the act of playing.

12

SPONTANEOUS BOUNCING OF THE BOW
Spiccato, Thrown Staccato, Sautillé

Staccato, as we have seen, involves conscious control of the bow. In spiccato, thrown staccato, or sautillé bowing, the tension of the bow does its own work. On the one hand the stress is on control—on the other it is on spontaneity. The feeling of spontaneity in the bow can best be developed by allowing it to bounce freely in the middle to tip area. The bow should be held loosely and dropped just above its mid-point 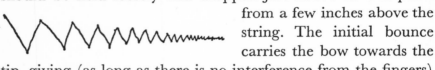 from a few inches above the string. The initial bounce carries the bow towards the tip, giving (as long as there is no interference from the fingers) a frequency graph similar to that in the diagram, of a rubber ball bouncing to a standstill.

Into this bounce a minimal control from the fingers can then be introduced, and with a delicate change of bow direction,

groups of notes can be isolated into simple rhythms. So fine is this control that it could be more accurately called restraint. The fingers simply contain and reflect each bounce at a given height with the sleight of hand of a conjurer. Mastery over such rhythms played at different speeds illustrates very clearly how much can be accomplished by how little.

Spontaneous bouncing, with the fingers playing the same

restraining role can also be seen in so-called sautillé bowing. This can be approached in two ways, both of which depend upon the use of the point of balance—that point a little above the middle of the bow where there is a natural tendency for it to bounce on its own accord. The first way of achieving sautillé bowing is to start from slowly articulated spiccato notes played alternately down and up: these increase speed and go through a difficult transition before giving way to a final spontaneity. The point of transition when the bow is neither one thing nor the other, neither controlled nor spontaneous, is well known to players—but not to all conductors, whose awkward tempos in such a passage as this in Rossini's *Thieving Magpie* Overture, show

little understanding of the problem. In the second way sautillé bowing is approached by playing short fast notes on the string at the point of balance. If the hand and fingers offer no interference, a natural tension between bow and string builds up to produce a spontaneous lift. In both methods, efficiency is increased by using little bow and playing nearer to the bridge than the fingerboard.

Spontaneity should be exploited fully. The greater the degree of spontaneity achieved, the greater will be the emphasis on bowing of an opposite nature. All opposites serve this end of reciprocal emphasis. Moreover it is the art of non-interference that ultimately allows that delicate balance where the bow does its own work and the instrument plays itself.

13

VIBRATO—THE LIFE RHYTHM

Its significance

Though so far vibrato has been left out of the picture, we must now stake for it a very important claim. We have seen the right arm as the expression of the will and the left hand as the articulator of form. But by themselves these factors are incomplete: the Franck Sonata for instance played with only energy and precision would have very little effect upon an audience. It would lack warmth from the heart. The same lack would be felt in a man who in his life worked only from logic or untempered drive. He would be described as having no feeling for his fellow men.

On a cosmic scale this situation could be likened to a body in space dying through lack of a vitalising force. Vibration is this vitalising force and exists wherever life incarnates in a given form. Each form has its own periodicity of vibration, whether it is a planet's revolution around the sun or the life span of a man or an insect, and within that periodicity, its own emotive pattern. The life process is, in fact, a system of vibrations constantly being recharged and sustained, and it is this pulsating heart of movement and circulation, sometimes referred to as the *third force*, which relates Father to Son, the power to the intellect, and completes the trinity of forces in the universe.

In terms of the violin, the power expressed through the right arm, in opposition to the articulation of form in the left hand, is balanced by such a vibration, which we call vibrato. Energy alone would be insensitive and articulation alone would be cold. As in the make-up of the human being, where there is a constant feeling assessment going on between the energy department and the intellectual control of that energy, this middle area is one of adaptability and movement. To it belong all the other aesthetic devices used in the performance of music—accelerandos and ritardandos, portamentos, fluctuations of forte and piano, and shaping of phrases—all of which, like vibrato itself, are too sensitive to be written down. For the string player we can say that though all are important, vibrato is supremely so: without it tone would be devoid of feeling and interest, and the more sensitive it is the more shades of feeling can be expressed and the more beauty will the music have.

It is interesting to observe the actual construction of the arm and the function of its parts, because the three-fold division is very clear and is a pointer to the claim that is to be made about the source of vibrato. The upper arm has one large bone, which corresponds with its function to express raw energy—as when an antagonist is punched to the ground: the forearm

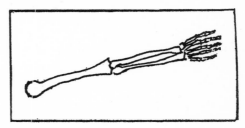

consists of two bones, which corresponds with the ambivalence of feeling in that their movement allows the palm of the hand to adopt emotive gestures—as turning upwards for acceptance and downwards for rejection: and the hand is broken up into fingers, which correspond with their function to carry out work of a precise and delicate nature. Of the other parallels to be found in the body, the most obvious is its own broad three-fold division— sub-diaphragmatic or energy department, single in its intent as the bone of the upper arm is single; chest or feeling area where the lungs correspond to the two bones of the forearm; and head, where the intellect and the five sense organs are closely allied and correspond to the five fingers. In fact, the three-fold division is a universal one and can be seen equally in the flower, the tree, the shape of a man's life and in the violin bow itself.

Seen in this way, and considering what was said earlier about right and left, the functions of the parts of the arm of the violinist can be seen in the following way. (Are there not relationships here too with the conductor's technique and more generally with the arms of the pianist and even the painter?)

RIGHT ARM: *Upper arm*—used for sustained weight and for power in attack, especially near the heel.

Hand—breaks up and patterns basic power, as in staccato and in passages requiring delicacy of control— notably from the fingers.

Forearm—used for carrying out a fluctuating and adaptable legato linking the other extremes—expresses feeling rather than power or precision.

LEFT ARM: *Upper arm*—relatively inactive since power is essentially a function of the right arm.

Hand—function centred in the fingers which articulate the form of the music—great precision necessary.

Forearm—counters the aridity of the fingers by imbuing them with life i.e. vibrato.

If the logic of this is understood it can be seen how the forearm is necessarily the source of vibrato since its function is connected with feeling. It is only necessary to listen critically to a relentlessly tight finger vibrato or an unyielding wrist wobble to see the truth in this. The reason for the inefficiency of both these types of vibrato is simply that they are a confusion of function. At the same time, however, we have to allow that in any field there are those few individuals who can achieve a high standard whilst breaking the rules and, because of this, dogmatism must be avoided. But for most people a vibrato which has been approached solely from the fingers or the wrist frequently ends in mechanical trouble and in a noticeable lack of beauty of tone. There is little danger of this if the approach has been made through the forearm. As we have seen, the essential quality of vibrato and of aesthetics in general is adaptability—the alternation between flatness and intensity and between coldness and passionate warmth. This ability to vary vibrato comes more naturally to the freer movement of the forearm than to the smaller and more restricted movement of the fingers.

It is also true that at certain times, for instance at moments of intensity or when the hand is in a high position on the lower strings the movement of the forearm merges with that of the fingers; but it can only do so with impunity once the essential movement of the forearm has been mastered.

The variability of vibrato

Vibrato consists of a sharpening and a flattening of the pitch of a note, the degree of which to some extent determines the degree of interest aroused. But by itself this does not give intensity. Another factor is necessary to give intensity to a violinist's tone, and this is, of course, the frequency of the vibration. It could be said that to widen the vibration increases the warmth of a note; that to increase the frequency increases its urgency; but that only by using both together can a true emotional intensity be achieved. In their interplay these two factors determine interest in a string player's tone, and one of the reasons why so much vibrato fails to give maximum impact is because only one of these possibilities is used; they are not controlled and varied significantly. Nothing is more boring than a vibrato which is on the one hand constantly narrow or wide or on the other hand slow or fast. It is the same for an actor: he can only hold interest by a play between the pitch and the speed of delivery of his words.

The different shades of emotional emphasis that can be achieved by varying the intensity pattern within a group of sustained notes is quite remarkable. In the simple melody *Plaisir d'Amour*, four patterns have been indicated, each one

producing a different character and feeling. How many more subtleties would be possible with the two factors of width and frequency varied: and how much could be gained by the ability to return to a 'flat' note and to reanimate it by any quality of vibrato at will. It can be seen too, that the patterns in the example could equally well apply to dynamics—so that there would then be three factors contributing to the shape of the music. But this does not mean that interest depends upon a loud dynamic: all three factors can be used in permutation and a different quality of intensity can be achieved by using the same vibrato at a *piano* level.

In quicker music, to vary vibrato during individual notes is relatively impracticable. We are now concerned with the degree of its intensity from one note to another, and even more with its total elimination. In this theme from the Mozart D major

Concerto, where there is a natural stress on the appoggiaturas, to vibrate every note, or every note equally, would destroy the effect of this stress, and anticipate the final appoggiatura on the F# and the sustained warmth on the G. There would be no sense of urging towards the head of a phrase. But equally, too little vibrato, or vibrato in the wrong places, would give no sense of the phrase being built up to a climax. In the example, unmarked notes suggesting no vibrato at all, and the size of the crosses indicating the degree of intensity in the vibrato, are the broadest indications towards a successful shaping of the phrase.

Similarly, at the opening of the Bach A minor Concerto, if every note is played with an equally intense vibrato, the A and F crotchets lose their point and the shape of the phrase is weakened. The quavers could well be played without vibrato. The stress on the last two quavers also will have little effect unless the groups of semiquavers are played with mathematical precision.

Another example of the close relationship between vibrato and phrase shape can be seen at times when it is necessary to sustain an uninterrupted flow over a bar-line or at the end of a bow. In

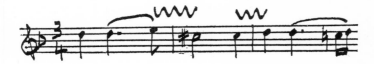

the example given from Corelli's *La Follia* sonata, vibrato at the marked places carries intensity through from one note to the next and guards against the common fault of breaking the line of the phrase at the end of the bow.

When vibrato should be used, and how much should be used, are two of the indefinables of playing: every individual will approach the same notes differently, and rules cannot be made. And yet it must paradoxically be studied with the greatest of care. The control of vibrato gives access to a tremendously wide range of feeling, and a player should be its master, able to summon it, cut it out, and control its quality at will. It is the great prize of the string player—the prize that differentiates him from all other instrumentalists. The pianist (who must have listened so often to accounts of the deficiencies of his instrument) can only feel frustration at not being able to mould a note once it has been struck. Other aesthetic devices employed by him cannot adequately make up for this basic lack: they cannot replace the supreme gift of the violinist of being able to change emotive colour every second his bow is on the string.

For this reason, the mechanics of vibrato deserve respectful attention from the very beginning. They should not be allowed to grow arbitrarily over the years creating havoc in the other departments of playing, however well those may have been mastered.

The mechanics of vibrato

There are three conditions to a successful forearm vibrato. The first is that a straight line should be maintained from the elbow to the knuckles with no bending at the wrist; the second is that there should be free and flexible movement at the elbow joint; the third is that the fingers should not press down too hard on the string—they should be firm yet pliable enough to allow the roll on the finger end. The final vibrato can best be reached by going through a series of preparatory movements.

A. To establish the basic flexibility required at the elbow, the arm, in playing position, is drawn lightly towards and away from the body.

B. Movement A is transferred to the instrument. The hand with the fingers in a group on one string, moves lightly up and down the fingerboard, gradually reducing the distance covered to about a tone.

C. The bow is now used. One finger—say, the second—still within the context of the forearm unit moving flexibily from the elbow, makes a moderately slow unbroken glissando of first a tone and then a semi-tone.

D. The compass of the glissando is reduced to a quarter-tone, and is at this point, on the edge of vibrato proper.

E. The transition is made. The finger ceases its quarter-tone oscillation, remaining firmly in one place on the string, but, at the same time, the forearm carries on the movement it was making in D. This gives rise to the roll on the finger and which constitutes vibrato.

The system of achieving vibrato having been established, the fingers should be exercised separately, varying the frequency and width of movement whilst maintaining regularity in vibration. It is important to aim at regularity because it is this that gives warmth to tone whereas irregularity produces hardness. Care must also be taken that neither the finger nor the thumb tighten on the neck of the instrument: if this happens, regularity is quickly lost. The device of holding the scroll against a wall or on a music stand is of use in this respect—it relieves anxiety about holding the violin and helps to clarify the mechanics. It shows particularly the pivoting of the finger against the ball of the thumb, and the need for space between the hand and the neck of the instrument. But whatever device is employed, the consequence of the continual use of a steely finger vibrato can not be dispersed magically; much hard work and patience will be necessary before warmth can be achieved.

14

INTEGRATED PLAYING

MUCH HAS BEEN said in the previous chapter in explanation of the three-fold division of a human being. We have said that a violinist expresses will through the right arm, intellectual precision through the left hand, and feeling through vibrato in the forearm: but what has not yet been considered is the need for the integration of these three departments.

Our judgement of players is made in phrases like 'a moving performance', 'terrifically powerful', 'technically good but it left me cold', and so on—all of which reflect an individual bias in one department or other. It is sometimes said however that a player 'has everything', which is a reference to the fact that power, technique, and feeling are there in equal quantities—that they have been integrated. When this occurs, it seems as though all who have heard such a performance are of the same mind: regardless of personal preference, they have all been drawn into the spell. These occasions are rare.

One of the aims of the teacher, however, should be to recognise the disbalance in a student of the three parts, and to make him aware of the possibility of balance through development. But this is not easy. Are we to say that the playing needs to be changed or that the individual himself needs to be changed? The two are clearly inseparable: outer reflects inner. In the same way that a gesture, a facial expression, a word, or a painter's canvas, are all outer forms of an inner reality, so a musician's playing is an unerring reflection of his inner self. All that he is can be found there.

The issue has, in fact, to be seen from the outside and the

inside at the same time. To force a change externally might merely draw out a capacity for imitation: in this case his *outer* would not correspond to his *inner* and his playing would be in danger of sounding unconvincing. Such forcing of the outer out of correspondence with the inner can only be the cause of breakdown. Many a youngster has disappeared from the limelight through subsequent failure to develop inwardly. On the other hand, to force a change internally is an impossibility. An individual may be guided, but change must come from within himself—he can only develop at his own speed.

Thus the process of teaching awareness and integration of the three departments of his being, in relation to his playing, is a sensitive play between inner and outer: external change must go hand in hand with a gentle education from the inside. This leading out process, or e-ducation, is the proper definition of all education. For inner and outer to work together is the surest way of laying sound roots for development: and it is the same process for the violinist as it is for the poet or the painter—it concerns the whole man and takes a lifetime.

Let us look again at the three aspects of man's being. One of the difficulties encountered in their co-ordination is the present day over-stress upon the faculty of reason. Man's logical mind tends to rule his life and is in constant movement and distracted activity: he is pressurised into specialisation and into assimilating facts for qualification purposes, so that in the West at least, man has lost touch with his source of immediate power. But this does not mean to say that the mind is not to be used—the exact science of a thing must be known, even if only as a stage in a whole process. Nor does it mean to say that a well trained mind or a perfect technique come to him easily: both have to be worked for, and every aspect of his task studied until he is able to see dependent parts of a whole structure and formulate a rationale of what he is doing. Many things stand in the way of this, but one stands out above the others—that is, undisciplined emotion.

As in life chaotic emotion hinders the capacity for clear thought, so in playing does it destroy clarity and purity of style. Excessive vibrato and wallowing in feeling should not be allowed to stand in the way of analysis during study—no amount of this can compensate for a lack of technical assurance.

In fact what is normally seen and understood as feeling is mechanical stuff. It is simply a preference of one thing to another in terms of like and dislike, or, in the conflict between the 'yes' of will and the 'no' of reason, it is seen as an unresolved turmoil of movement. It is then more accurately called emotion or e-motion, a movement out, which like an unbridled horse charges out of control in this direction and that. Such emotional disturbances are reflected in playing as gushes of sound, instability of tempo and in an arbitrary use of vibrato, all of which interfere with natural phrasing of the music in the same way that fear interferes with the natural rhythm of breathing. For this there is no easy remedy. Development of feeling is a subtle process which involves the individual's evaluation of his own relationship with his fellow men and the universe. Such sensitivity can only come of life itself and results in a rare compassion. For this reason real sensitivity in playing is more often than not the last quality to develop. And when it does so it can not be pre-determined, for as we have seen its expression as beauty is essentially adaptable and can not be expressed in the same way in any two individuals. Moreover, no individual within himself will feel the same from one minute to the next. Yet without this element, as all musicians know, all the energy and technique in the world is ineffectual.

Animal drive, or pure energy, whichever way we look at it, has been discussed already in the chapters on power and the right arm. As we have said, the biggest issue here is that the energy should be allowed to express freely. Uninhibited and wholly efficient use of energy is rare—on two counts. Firstly we have spoken of the physical body and the gravity pulls which restrict it on its own level, and secondly there are the psychological factors—the do's and dont's, self consciousness of the wrong sort, and fears, all of which inhibit its free flow. Again, it is only by becoming aware of these inhibiting forces that progress can be made: to do this and to find the causes of limitation is always a challenge. The energy of which we speak is the creative power both in the universe and in man; with the power of an explosion it can shock people out of their ordinary inert state into one of identification with the player—or rather with the supra-personal forces working through him. Free energy is indispensible to the performing artist.

The different modes of power working within a human being can be approached in varying ways. It is, for instance, possible to relate them to the four elements as anciently used and as found in modern astrology, where fire, air, water and earth all express themselves in individuals according to their particular constitution. Even here, a close affinity will be found with our three-fold concept. Fire can be seen as will or energy working through earth—that is the physical body; air corresponds to the activities of the head—the acquiring of a technique; and water corresponds to feeling in all its aspects. The three-fold image is used in this book because it offers a guiding concept about integration which is universal and can apply to all activities whatever. It is a process of exhausting all analytical possibilities —that is technique, in order that power may flow through that technique without hindrance, and of vitalising the whole by a pulsating life of feeling. Only when in some degree this three-fold integration is realised will another being be moved in a complete sense by a performance.

15

SOME COMMON WEAKNESSES

Leakage of energy

The style of many violinists is spoiled by effortful and uneasy gestures. Such gestures are not only unnecessary but dangerous: they can beguile a player into believing that they are indispensable, and, once established resist removal tenaciously. Fundamentally they are compensations for unsolved technical problems: that is to say that energy which should have had a constructive use has leaked into wrong channels. Again we are concerned with the minimal amount of energy required to achieve a given result—in fact, with the beauty of economy.

A common example of such a leakage of energy is the facial grimace which occurs when say a bowing problem is particularly troublesome. Ultimately the grimace will become so indispensable to that particular problem that if a player is asked to remove it, his control will fall to pieces. A similar compensatory movement is the swing of the violin to the left which arises when the bow arm becomes locked at the shoulder as the heel is approached, conveniently finishing off the undone work of the arm. Again if a player is asked to remove the swing, his bow control will be badly affected. Or, as a final example we can take the beating of time by the body and often by the bow-arm as it plays. Rhythmic control not having been inwardly mastered, the body often makes energetic attempts to take over the role of time keeper. Asked to still his body, a player will again lose control. A return to an economic use of the body can only be made by first of all recognising a wasteful movement, and then studying the function of the relevant part of the body and eliminating all movement that does not help to fulfil that function. The process of elimination must be done with stillness of mind and body: irritable gestures to be seen in practice rooms will not produce fruit. The feeling of losing all one ever had, once the false begins to give way to the true, is equivalent to the psychological distress felt when certain aspects of personality are being shed that have been recognised as false and valueless. It has to be seen as a necessary stage in the rediscovery of purity.

'When in doubt, leave out'

There is a defence mechanism known in the orchestral world as, when in doubt, leave out. Its use soon becomes second nature at moments of indecision and has saved many a player his job. Unfortunately, this mechanism also finds its way into the practice room. In its simplest form it is to be seen in the upper reaches of scales and arpeggios where there is a sudden drop in dynamic level, a slowing down of tempo, and a loss of freedom in use of the bow until safe ground is reached. All this is of course a camouflage for inefficiency, and there is only one counter to it—to practice both assimilated and unassimilated passages together at the same reduced tempo and at the same dynamic, until the problem can be approached confidently at the correct tempo. In the practice room, the saying should be reversed to: 'when in doubt, play out.'

The lost last beat

This issue has to some extent already been seen in the chapter on legato. It concerns the tendency to overindulge the beginning of a bow stroke and to lose power at the end of it. In the Leclair *Sarabande*, for instance, the notes crossed in the illustration,

tend to lose intensity instead of carrying the phrase over the bar-line. To overcome this, the first half of the bow should be conserved in order to allow expansion in the second; this means, in fact, a slight disbalance in the division of the bow so that the second part of each slur is given slightly more than half the bow. The string player should always feel that he still has room to breathe at the end of his bow and should realise that conservation of the bow at the beginning of a note whether from the heel or the tip is essential to the feeling of freedom at the bow change. This should be regarded, more than it is, as a fundamental aspect of bow control. As a well trained voice conveys the impression of a continual reserve of breath, so a bow should convey the impression of having no end.

Which part of the bow?

No violinist would attempt to play the opening of the 'Hunt' Quartet near the tip of the bow for the simple reason that the particular quality of lift and the control required are only to be found in the lower half. Similar comments could be made on any passage of music—style, dynamics, speed and rhythm, all add up to determine a specific point on the bow where it can be played most efficiently. Why is it then, that so many players appear to be glued to the limited area between middle and tip, and avoid the lower six inches near the heel. Mechanical causes of this have already been discussed. But another factor in this is the failure to realise, during the years of training, that only one part of the bow has a true correspondence with one effect. This aspect of bow control is so sensitive and has such a wide range, that no attempt will be made to study it in detail here. The student should see for himself, as he progresses, that true control can be measured in inches. What student has realised this and taken a page of a Mozart piano trio to work out with logical precision the exact placing of every note? All music should be approached in this way until arbitrariness in the use of the bow is eliminated. Control is beautiful to the eye: there can be no more satisfying sight than that of a bow being used with equal ease at every point of its length.

Though there is no short cut to this control, one exercise can be suggested which helps to develop facility in all parts of the bow. These notes, taken from Fiocco's *Allegro* are played in turn

in each quarter, first, second, third, fourth, and then back through fourth, third, second and first, all without break. The aim is to achieve such an evenness of tone that a listener is unable to distinguish in which part of the bow it is being played.

Forced tone

One of the most common dangers in playing is what is referred to as forcing the tone. It is true that most students have to suffer inadequate instruments and that the effort to produce a powerful sound out of them causes much of this forcing. But it is more likely to be a compensation for something else—a weak left hand or a poor vibrato, or more directly, wrong control in the arm itself. Whatever the cause, there is a common misapprehension that the right arm rights all wrongs and is totally responsible for quantity of sound: consequently the error of trying too hard kills the very vibrancy of tone it sets out to achieve. Nothing but hardness of tone comes from an arm that tries to wrest intensity out of every note.

Work must be done, therefore, on the right arm itself, but a device can also be used which helps to minimise the whole sense of making effort. This is to transfer attention completely from the right arm to the left hand, concentrating either upon precision or warmth of vibrato according to the nature of the passage. If at the same time the aim has lightly been set of allowing the bow to move effortlessly over the strings, quality of tone can be made to soar in the air. A parallel can be made to the intellect wrestling with a problem until it finds itself at a total impasse. Once intensity of effort is released and the attention is moved elsewhere, a spontaneous answer to the problem often presents itself.

If the exercise is carried out correctly, further proof will not be needed that warmth of tone depends a great deal upon the left hand, and that more often than not, the right arm is guilty of over-exertion.

Identification with the bits

There is a tendency among students to treat individual notes or groups of notes separately without first referring them to the context of a whole phrase. When an artist paints a portrait, it is useless for him to start with a hand or an ear; he must first see the whole and work from the whole to the parts. The nearer he is to a visualisation of the intended result, the nearer will he be to a successful work of art. In the realm of ideas, too, much error is caused through identification with partial truths: the statement, for instance, 'he is a weak man', could be the source of much misunderstanding unless related to wider concepts. Similarly, the musician should be concerned with the whole, mentally imaging the widest possible phrase shape within which a series of notes may be held, and even further the relationship of one phrase to another. Only when such shapes are held in mind can the bits be tackled: technical issues such as bow control, note values, dynamics, and so on, can then be seen in their right perspective.

16

INTONATION PROBLEMS

Problems of intonation are either physical or mental. The physical ones have already been touched upon in previous chapters. Two of them stand out: sluggishness in the left elbow, which impedes the easy movement of the hand over the finger-board, and excessive pressure by the fingers upon the strings, which impedes the necessary flexibility for making high speed adjustments to notes struck initially out of tune. In fact all that has been said about the body in general and the left hand in particular applies to problems of intonation: we are again concerned with tension states and adequate nervous response.

The mental issues are to do with simply *listening*. It may seem naïve to assert that bad intonation is caused by a player not listening to what he plays. But so often this is the case. To listen requires attention, and attention (discussed more fully in the next chapter) is easily dispersed, destroying the value of the work being done. Unless during the early years, the practice of holding attention during a note is established, so that a sense of being exactly in tune is developed, the ill effects of approximating accumulate until *very near* is taken for *accurate*. The player is then not aware that he is out of tune—he is not even listening. There is a hitting power and a sheer beauty of sound in a note played exactly in tune and this must be recognised and sought from the very beginning.

If intonation is to be re-thought, therefore, it should be from the point of view of attention: a player must be exactly *there* whilst a note is being played. Normal methods of checking against open strings and harmonics, and the use of the *difference tone* can then be applied to full advantage. The difference tone can be singled out as an extremely acute method of checking intonation. The audible third note that results when two notes are played together, only resonates freely when the two sounded notes are micro-tonally accurate. Fourths, thirds and sixths found in adjacent notes should be played as intervals, at a forte dynamic and sustained without vibrato, until through adjustment, the difference tone (marked in brackets) sings out clearly and accurately.

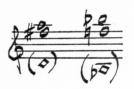

Intonation in the higher positions can of course be helped by guide notes: these, usually on the first or second fingers, so as to facilitate a jump made to the third or fourth fingers, are a stock-in-trade of the violinist and scarcely need a mention. Their success depends upon a closely knit unity in the hand and upon the speed at which the move can be made. They also work more efficiently if they are part of the harmonic structure of a passage, so that subsequent notes within that structure lie under the hand. On the same basis, the first finger should whenever possible, remain down on the string to give a sense of security to the fingers as they shift from position. In the actual marking of music, only those fingers indicating a change of position should find their way into the part, and these should be decisive and clear to read. Lines extending from one fingering to the next help by giving a clear indication that the hand should stay firmly in that position until the next shift. But for the left hand to be able to work with the faultlessness of a machine in all parts of the fingerboard, familiarity with positions is essential. The ability to move with facility across the strings in any position should be high on the list of a student's aims. A book of studies such as Campagnoli's *Divertissements* is invaluable to this end.

Finally it should be restated that when checking intonation in any one of the available methods, it is essential that vibrato should be eliminated: much self-delusion goes on under the camouflage of vibrato. Bow strokes should be loud and sustained and the notes expressionless so that they can be acutely examined.

17

ATTENTION AND METHOD IN PRACTICE

IT IS EXTREMELY difficult to establish method in a student's practice. Too often, practice is simply seen as a question of 'how many hours have I put in?' The amount of time has in fact little to do with a desired result: far too much time is spent in arbitrary and uneconomic playing which is then described as serious study.

The greatest hindrance to efficient work is the difficulty common to all human beings of sustaining concentration. Anyone who has the slightest knowledge of meditative procedures will know the extreme difficulty of holding awareness in the present moment of time: they will have seen the mind running to and fro between past and future and between 'yes' and 'no', unable to contain itself in the *here and now*. They will also know that when attention is dissipated in this way, work done is virtually useless. For this reason, long periods of uninterrupted work are unproductive. The amount of time in them of real attention is very small and it is better as a general rule that work should consist of short periods done with attention and frequent breaks for relaxation. This must be so because everything in nature, including the activity of the mind, is phasic in its behaviour. The aim, therefore, to do six hours of 'solid practice', should be abandoned as a misunderstanding of human mechanics.

The idea, too, of getting to grips with or getting one's teeth into a problem should also be abandoned. Such an attitude precludes attention which is essentially light and unaggressive. It also involves the body in tensions and extravagances that have no value in the solving of a technical problem. Attention is a holding of awareness from moment to moment upon a given point—it is not the screwing up of the forehead or the gritting of the teeth in intense effort. In this sense, attention is closely related to that part at the deepest level within a human being which is able detachedly to observe the activities going on within his organism. This observer is an unbiased eye which does not identify with a situation and is able to hold full consciousness of it. It is, in fact, the eternal lying behind and within all men—a treasure rarely uncovered because of external and temporal pressures in life.

As the external world is a maya which holds a human being spellbound, so the written page in music tends to hold the player spellbound and is therefore an enemy of attention. When the eye looks at the music the danger is that it becomes locked in the music—that there is only a one-way flow of energy, from the perceiver to the perceived. This state of affairs can often be seen in a student hard at work—the eyes give the appearance of being riveted to the music and it is clear that there can be no real awareness of the problem being studied. For this reason, the use of music should be approached with care. In learning a piece or studying a given problem, a group of notes should be established in the memory as soon as possible, and whenever the eye is allowed to follow the music, it should do so on the slenderest of threads and always be on the edge of being released.

The opening of the Beethoven 'Spring' Sonata will suffice as a

model for study. The object here let us say, is the analysis of three aspects of the bow—the use of the whole bow, its uniform division into parts, and the maintaining of an even dynamic. The passage has been memorised and work is being done in slow motion. Attention is kept alert from moment to moment as described, and the eye lightly follows the movement of the bow over the string. But how long can such a high level of attention be held before the mind invades, reliving an earlier happening in the day or turning over an unresolved personal problem—or the eye is distracted by a face moving past a window or a headline of a newspaper lying nearby.

Though it is difficult for attention to be sustained in this way, when reached it is essentially simple. That is to say there is nothing external to it which hinders an absolutely clear vision, and because of this it has the power to cut through so-called problems. Once approached with this clarity of vision a problem ceases to be a problem, and for this reason two minutes work done with attention are worth two hundred done with the mind in a state of daydream. Such slow motion analysis is of course only a means to an end: it has to be thrown away when its analytical purpose has been fulfilled. The studied gestures of the actor must in performance be opened up to free energy and the feeling demands of the situation, and as we have seen in the chapter *Integrated Playing*, the violinist, having practiced with scientific attention to difficulties, must then throw them out of the window. If the result is still unsatisfactory, there is still analytical work to be done.

The question may be asked as to what material should be studied in relation to the ideas put forward in this book. The answer is that any bar of music from anywhere is useful for someone. All creators of violin schools have been aware of the same fundamental problems: a study is only an extended abstraction of one aspect of technique and parallels can be found from one study book to the next. But all problems whatever can be found in the Beethoven and Mozart string quartets. What is important is not whether Spohr, de Bériot, Rode,

Fiorillo or Mazas should be consulted, but whether the principles that underlie all violin playing have been understood. If they have, and a specific need has been correctly assessed, then the whole of music is open to choice.

As a final word on practice methods, the use of the tape machine can be encouraged as a modern aid. Its value lies in the unwillingness of the individual to observe himself clearly. The weaknesses and idiosyncracies of others hit us with terrible clarity whilst our own are all too often swept under the carpet. Not only are they hidden there because they are too painful to see, but they are defended when attacked—a truth known to all husbands, wives and violin teachers. There is no film in life to play back our weaknesses to us, but on the violin they can be recorded and heard as though they belonged to another person. Comments from teachers that have been doubted may be verified. Does vibrato die before the end of a note; do odd notes stand out disrupting phrasing; is intonation as true as it was imagined; are the rests shortened destroying the rhythm? The played back tape is an unerring ear and is therefore of great value to a student.

18

THE ROLE OF BREATHING

IN AN OVERALL picture of the body, where the key word is expansion, the process of breathing can not be forgotten: it would be illogical, for instance, if while working at lightness and free movement in the right arm, the body itself felt deflated and heavy through lack of air. There is an obvious correspondence between certain psychic states and the breath: the *inspiration* of the artist is clearly related to the inspiration of air; the elevating effect of breath is reflected in the word *aspiration*; and conversely despair is expressed as an outbreath accompanied by a general heaviness of the body—and so on. This relationship of breath and feeling is well known to the singer whose art depends upon the manipulation of breath according to the emotive content of the words.

Obviously the violinist is not primarily concerned with breath —he breathes with his bow: in fact his art consists of simulating with his bow the natural flow of the singer's breath through the ends of notes, and shaping a phrase through the sensitive control of its pressure. Even so it is at times a help to be conscious of the breath itself. There is no better medicine for a cramped body or a tense mind than to begin a period of study with this simple exercise. An inbreath is taken immediately at the beginning of the harmonic, reaches its climax during the rests and falls in

readiness for the next note. At the same time, as the bow leaves
the string, it is made to draw a circle in the air as described in
Movement 5 in the chapter on the right arm. In this way, lightness of the arm, lightness in the lungs, and circulation, all work
together to the same end.

A variation on the previous exercise shows how breath can
relate to the equality of the sound. When the breath is held

lightly during the second bar in the example, the required
flautando sound seems to come to the bow more naturally. On
the other hand, the same notes played aggressively require that

the lungs should be filled quickly before the bar line in order to
prepare for the next attack. Would any player consider making
the attack at the opening of the Bartok Concerto with deflated
lungs? To do so would be out of correspondence with the natural
need of the body.

Rules cannot be made; phrases are often very long and do not
essentially correspond with the fluctuations of the breath. But in
long sustained melodies, however, breathing and phrasing should
when possible be allowed their natural tendency to correspond.
In the Bach Air from the Suite in D, the progression from the
low A to the high A, calls for a correspondingly expansive

inbreath. Or in other cases the general level of expansiveness in the breathing can be raised according to a more general

intensity in the music, as in the quoted fortissimo climax in the Franck Sonata.

There is no intention to overstress this relationship between breathing and phrasing—or the need for too meticulous work upon it. Breathing must remain a natural process and the marking of breathing places in the music, for instance, is not advocated. This would give an undue stress to the whole issue. The object has been to suggest that breathing has both an artistic and a therapeutic value. Not only should it be considered by those who are naturally heavy in body and in style, but also by those who are beset by fear, for at such times the freeing of constricted breathing can go a long way to freeing parallel constrictions in the body. If our music making, as all art, is as we have previously claimed man's attempt to return to the infinite, it must be upwards against gravity that the spirit soars. The breath symbolises that soaring spirit and deserves careful consideration.

19

OPPOSITES CONSIDERED

LIFE INTEREST is directly dependent upon a play between opposites. The emergence of hope in the middle of despair, success in failure or love out of hate, all give rise to a tension without which life would fall flat. An actor's art is in manipulating such opposites so that an audience is never certain in which direction it is being led. A violinist may not have words at his disposal but he too has the power to hold an audience on a tightrope through his own particular manipulation of opposites. Let us look at the ways in which he may do this.

Firstly there are the universal opposites to be found in any field—bondage and the licence to do whatever one feels which is erroneously called freedom. Though excessive bondage is death, excessive licence is not freedom but chaos. Freedom lies between the two: in the word itself lies a subtle reference to the fact that real freedom comes from the *free* working within the *dome*. For the player, freedom is not an anarchic release from the the bondage of the bar-line but a subtle note to note flexibility which works within and transcends them. Such freedom is seen in the whole creative process where the free spirit, in bondage to matter, moves deviously within it to avoid captivity. This deviousness is entirely unpredictable. Even in the laws of mathematics, in the structure of harmonics, and in the well-tempered scale, there is always something that does not quite fit.

Art has the same unpredictability—the same itching to avoid confinement. It is man's attempt to return through beauty to the infinite: the aesthetic sense, as we have seen before, is adaptable and unpredictable, reconciling the opposites of free will and bonded intellect. Freedom—or beauty—for the performing musician, is the sensitive avoidance of restrictions that the beats and bar-lines would impose upon him. Such 'inaccuracies'— the holding back or urging forward of individual notes or groups of notes—are the unspeakable in music. If a composer were to include all he hears when he conceives his compositions, the pages of music would be black with print: he would also restrict the uniqueness of the individual performances. The written page is therefore the merest guide to the playing of music. We do not need to ask what a group of notes, as these

from the Mozart D major Concerto, would sound like if played exactly as written.

Another aspect of the free and the bound is the player's relationship with his instrument. We have seen this elsewhere as a play between control and spontaneity. A delicate balance must be found between the effort from the player to play and the need of the instrument to play itself. As a human being hinders his understanding by an excess of his own personality, so a player inhibits the potential of his instrument by trying to force it to speak. His instrument wants to speak without his help: the acquiring of a technique is only a means of allowing this to happen.

Dynamics may be thought too commonplace to be considered as opposites: but the range of sound between as loud as possible and as soft as possible is in itself capable of expressing great changes in feeling. Dynamics are particularly relevant to Western man, who although intellectually stressed has within him an unresolved violence. His extroversion and his individualism have led to the expression of this conflict whether it is seen as light and shade in painting, tragedy and comedy in the theatre, or forte and piano in music. Beethoven's violent dynamic changes are an indication of the intensity with which he wrestled with the opposites within him. On the other hand the more introverted and spiritual East reflects its psyche in monotonic musings with little stress on dynamic changes, and the so-called primitive peoples, who do not have the complication of the rational faculty to the same degree, are concerned with expressing the life pulse.

Since, then, a Western musician is unavoidably involved in expressing dynamics, he should be able to exploit the whole range, moving from one level to another with an immediacy unimpaired by anticipation: for anticipation is an enemy of vitality. First the expanding of the dynamic range out of the mezzo-forte level adopted by many students, and then sensitivity to immediacy. Both must be under control if the interest of an audience is to be held. The quartet music of Beethoven, especially passages from the slow movements, can be used for

study: the passage from Opus 59 No. 1 is given as typical of many.

Another way in which an instrumentalist can create interest through opposites, is by the full exploitation of the quality of different types of bowing. In juxtaposition different types of bowings are often insufficiently differentiated and the impact of both is lost. In this passage from the Mozart C major Sonata the

length of the crotchet B in the first bar and of the crotchet C in the second bar is often shortened, especially by cutting off vibrato too soon. To suggest any brevity in the quality of these notes anticipates the short staccato notes that follow, and thus contrast is lost. Equally the notes prior to the staccato quavers in the third bar must maintain their legato quality to the last moment, or again there is insufficient contrast. Similarly in the Brahms A major Sonata, the effectiveness of the short triplets is

lost unless the previous crotchets have been given their full length. In both examples we could reverse the situation and speak of the effect upon the sustained notes made by well articulated staccato notes. It is a process of reciprocal emphasis —one opposite affirms the other. String music is full of instances where interest depends upon such manipulation of opposites.

Similarly, but on a bigger scale, the actual character of the music itself should be exploited to the full. An obvious example would be when a hard percussive passage is followed by a flautando fingerboard passage: unless the change of character is registered fully, neither will be effective. In the same way, if the individual movements of a sonata are played on the same stylistic level, the totality of the sonata, which depends upon the formal and feeling differences inherent in each movement, will suffer. Finally, increasing our scale even further, if Bach, Franck, Sarasate, and Beethoven are to be played in the same programme, the unique character of each composer must be felt, and a player's own personality subjugated to the end of a full realisation of that uniqueness. The ability to move quickly between opposing styles calls for great adaptability from a performer: to exploit fully the idiomatic and feeling differences of consecutive pieces is to give each character by opposition.

Many other opposites can be found under different headings throughout this book. We have seen, for instance, that a secure balance lies in movement; that the bow and violin are male and female respectively; that efficient force from the bow arm depends upon a prior minimal tension state; and that the drive of the right arm is opposed by the formulatory function of the left hand. There are many others.

The whole field of music as of life itself is in fact a play of opposites, and if the tension between them is allowed to slacken, in the same instant, the vital interest of an audience will be lost.

20

THE PRICE OF THE SOLOIST

THE PRICE OF authority is responsibility, and the responsibility of being a top-ranking soloist is the constant application and specialisation necessary to maintain an achieved position. It is no mean price. Over-specialisation by the aspiring violinist is a danger even in the earliest student days. The concentration of effort upon one objective tends to preclude the wider development we have referred to previously. For a young child or an older student to be shut up in his room for long periods of time with the violin as his horizon, can be a hindrance to natural growth. Such an unnatural discipline has been enforced by many parents at the expense of the child, unless he is of the very rare variety that wishes to play for himself without pressure. There is something precious and over-protected about the aura surrounding a brilliantly talented young musician which separates him from his fellows and causes endless psychological difficulties later. Equally there is something lacking in a brilliant adult violinist whose only vocabulary concerns the violin.

Moreover, the struggle for self-realisation is an extremely long process and can produce a dangerously confined self interest of the wrong kind. Healthy self interest involves a deep knowledge of the self which aims at making the individual an instrument for the expression of a universal power. Otherwise it is merely the retention of personal gifts as private property, which produces among other things an inability to talk about anything but the programme for the next concert or the interpretative improvements in the last one. There is also the danger, in the pursuit of self-realisation, of an almost total denial of that part of life to do with human relationships. Sacrifices normally made in a marriage relationship or in any other situation demanding responsibility, are often viewed only as infringements upon personal time and liberty. These are conflicts attendant upon all artistic aspiration, and although by many great violinists they are transcended, in others they remain confused and unresolved.

The perfection of the finished performance, the ultimate mastery of the instrument, and the realised ambition have to be seen by the individual against such instances of the price of dedication.

21

FACING A PUBLIC

THE ABILITY to play well is one thing: the ability to demonstrate that ability to others is another. One is to do with conscious acquisition of technique—the other, more complex, is to do with the unconscious forces of fear working within a man. These unconscious inhibiting forces are so powerful that most musicians at some time or other in their lives have been undermined by them. They also account for why many talented players are never heard at all by the public, and why so many players achieve a fleeting recognition and are then never heard of again. Let us look at the two main sources of fear.

The fear common to all men is rooted in pride. A man's deepest motivating force is his pride—he has a deep egocentric need to prove himself superior to his neighbour and to this end a part of him secretly desires his neighbour's downfall. Any self-reflecting man may see this within himself: equally he will be able to see that the egotism in others secretly desires his own downfall. It is in fact a game of power in which the loss of that power is always at stake, and it is the fear of this loss of power that sets in motion the psychosomatic reactions that reduce efficiency and bring about its ultimate loss. Thus we have the all too well known vicious circle. Here is the inner struggle of a man: the idealism—the pure in him—aims at the perfection of whatever he has undertaken; but in the process, pride—the impure in him—interferes and sows the seed of failure.

Thus the soloist who can stand before a thousand people without turning a hair is either a naïve man with a gift, or a man who has gone into the experience that life has to offer, and after much self seeking has succeeded in returning to an inner simplicity. From such a simplicity, purified of personal colouring and self interest, there will be no interference from fear, and the music will appear to play itself. Such perfection is extremely rare and, for most men, some hairs have to be turned and the duality of can I, can't I, lives with them to some degree or other throughout their lives. A genius, who, as the word implies, is a man who has inherited the concentrated work of his ancestors, sets off in his unspoiled youth by spontaneously expressing his gift, but later he inevitably has to cross the bridge of analytical and egotistic thinking. Then the question is simply, will he be master of it, or it of him.

Unfortunately, to this element common to all men is added an individual element: emotional patterns, that have been laid down and have condensed during early childhood, make the picture more complex. Such patterns are the result of pressures from other individuals—specifically, parents. Partly due to the sociological background of the time, generating unfulfilled ambitions and a sense of 'wanting to give my child the chance I didn't have', many children have been unnaturally pressed to achieve greatness. Unrealistic ideas about music, fame and the image of the violin virtuoso have caused the violin to be much abused in this way.

Such pressures give rise to a great variety of results. Perhaps the least fortunate of them is that of a child possessing little or no natural talent, being forced to practise until his obvious inability to make good, conflicting with his desire to win the approbation of his parents, causes breakdown. Or a gifted child may have no desire to become a soloist but suffers such hurt protestations from the parents that guilt complexes of having let down the parents are built up. Or a child may be gifted but have such excessive pressure put on him to overcome all competition, that the slightest shortcoming may leave its mark for life. Or there is the danger, in the specialisation and the confinement from normal life entailed by long hours of practice, that a young person's natural development is hampered. Mental strain from the desire to be 'normal' may result in resentment and rejection of the instrument.

These, and many other variations of the relationship tensions in early childhood, stand in the way of the ability to play fearlessly later on; and their roots, buried under the level of normal consciousness, are not to be controlled by the rational mind. These roots can only be removed by the long process of self knowledge—by fully entering into areas of discomfort and by exposure to emotional replays of the situations that were the cause of the trouble.

In the immediate situation just before playing, only stillness of mind and body can have any ameliorating effect upon fear or tension. This can be helped by slow diaphragmatic breathing, if it is remembered that in a nervous condition breathing takes place too high in the chest which is consequently not oxygenated properly, causing the heart to beat faster. There is no greater help however than a mind that has undergone some form of training, and is able to still its vacillation between confidence and doubt.

It is often said that a player does not give of his best unless he is 'nervous'. It is of course true—although we cannot mean by this the nervous state resulting from the sort of fears which we have been discussing: these cause different degrees of paralysis and only impede control. But the nervous state which is a highly keyed, vibratory link between performer and audience is indispensable. It is the pre-condition of a vital performance. In it the highest degree of sensitivity of control is reached and the body acts with an immediacy not normally realised in human beings. Such an immediacy is usually only seen in emergency situations, as in a man who has to save himself from a burning building, or in a fugitive running for his life: then there is an alertness like that of the wild animal pricking its ears for the tell-tale crackle of a twig. It is a dangerous situation: and in a sense so is that of the performer. He can not afford to slacken tension or this alertness goes and with it the interest of his audience: as soloists well know the moment of greatest danger is the moment of complacency—the moment of slackened aware-ness. Any performer moreover who claims to be oblivious to this nervous tension when he walks on to a stage does not speak the truth: he defends himself unnecessarily, for it is the condition of his art. There can be no comparison between the best perfor-mance done in the solitude of the practice room to that done an hour later in the tension situation with an audience. In this sense, then, nerves do bring out the best in a player.

A few words can be said here about playing from memory. Speed of actual learning and power of retention, it is true, vary from person to person; nevertheless memorising is largely a question of quality of practice. Those who find it difficult should first examine their inability in terms of attention. The problem of memorising during performance has even more to do with maintaining a *here and now* awareness, for the tendency of the mind is to run ahead in anticipation and doubt. We are again in the realm of fear. The key word is immediacy, and all that has been said earlier on this subject appertains here, especially that in Chapter 9. The value of 'playing from mem-ory' is to be found in the sister expression 'playing by heart'. It suggests an understanding on a deep level—a penetration to the very heart of the music by the heart of the player. To achieve this communion it is doubtless better that the external eyes should be passive, for they represent *division*, and it is the singleness of the internal eye that allow the *vision* of the artist.

22

THE TRANSITION

THE PROCESS of growing up is nowhere more clearly marked than in the realm of art. There is a time of intense growth from the youth of seventeen to the man of thirty-five when he avidly searches for his true self and unburdens himself through his art, whether as soloist, painter, poet or composer. The process is a transition from idealism which is loosely equated with freedom, to reality which is loosely equated with bondage in a material world. To the student, idealism and reality seem poles apart: he feels that in committing himself to reality he will lose his so-called freedom. But as we have already seen in the chapter on opposites, freedom is wrongly understood—it really signifies the ability of the *free* to move within the *dome*, not a glorious sense of release from all material things. On the one hand, failure to come to terms with the material world produces a being who can neither relate to other beings, nor lead an ordered existence; and on the other hand for material security to absorb idealism, produces a being who has lost the quest for perfection. Nothing can be gained from taking refuge in a cave—nor can anything be gained from total identification with outer form.

How then is the violinist to find his own particular freedom in the transition from student to professional musician. Clearly only a handful of players will reach the first rank of artist performer, and many for the first time will sit in permanent orchestras and feel a sudden loss of individual identity. Others will teach and experience an all-round drop in the standard of playing to which they have been used. In both cases there will be a tendency to look back at the hours of work on the Mendelssohn, the Bach double, or the Bartok, and ask 'what use have they been?'

In the orchestral world, the sacrificing of the will to the will of a conductor can, to some, be a sore imposition upon the student freedom that has just been left. As in the parallel experience of marriage, the sacrifice can be painful, and unless it can be seen to have value, the desire to be free of it is soon all that remains (we then see the phenomenon of the disgruntled orchestral musician). Its value lies chiefly in the continued quest for perfection and the resolve to be a permanent student of one's instrument: it is possible even in orchestral life to get deep satisfaction from mastering technical problems. The value of such an experience lies also in a widening understanding of music and men—in the constant association with great music and great soloists: for who but the orchestral player can feel so intimately the physical thrill of the *Rite of Spring*, the technical virtuosity of *The Bartered Bride* Overture or the sensuousness of *Daphnis and Chloe*. The music is around him and floods his whole being. Or who more has the privilege of that rare magical solo performance (though he may not admit it when it happens) that re-establishes his faith not only in music but in life itself. Also, stemming from his orchestral experience, there is the possibility of a later and a more mature involvement in chamber music and solo work—not, as is so often assumed, an inevitable drift away from these activities. These positive aspects of orchestral life must be valued: they guard against the times that all players have been through when they feel that their role is little more than that of a musical clerk.

As for the teacher, his loss of freedom contains within it the possibility of a deeper understanding of human beings and of the subject he is teaching. He has the constant challenge of conveying meaning to individuals at widely different levels of understanding, and the need for continual re-clarification of his own ideas. Because of this the sensitivity of the teacher, if he allows it, can be sharpened to its limit—the pupil, as is often said, becomes his teacher. Thus his own particular quest for perfection is kept alive: once he is confident he knows all there is to know about his subject he is denying himself his own development.

If the transition from student to player or teacher is to be summed up therefore, it would be to say that the process of growth never ceases. The bondage which may be regarded initially with distaste is actually the necessary and inevitable framework for development.

23

CODA

BOOKS PURPORTING to describe physical actions can never be an adequate substitute for individual contact with a teacher, and moreover the most important things in the performance of music are beyond words or definition: many things therefore that could have been said have been left unsaid in this book. Nevertheless, if its logic has been followed, certain guides to achieving both technique and the undefinable mystery in performing will have emerged. We have gone back to first causes and built a structure in which all parts inter-relate with the intimacy of cog wheels in a delicate machine. Here, restated for clarity, are some of the wheels that make up this machine:

A feeling awareness in the body leading to a maximum degree of freedom of limb. An understanding of the dangers of contraction.

A stance which is dependant upon movement, spinal alignment, and the correct placing of the feet.

The law of right over left in which the function of the bow and violin determines their position and that of the body.

The imaging of the violin and bow as female and male that work together harmoniously through a sensitive mutual relationship.

The function of the right arm, left hand and vibrato related to the three universal forces of will, intellect, and feeling.

A new concept of holding the bow in which minimal interference from the fingers allows spontaneity in the bow.

The term *pressure* avoided: power in the right arm seen as weight plus movement: the beneficial effect of circular movement: the importance of considering the properties of a vibrated string.

Power related to the animal kingdom: the attack of the violinist seen as a three-fold process depending upon the absence of contraction in the arm.

Difficulties of legato seen to be dependent upon relaxation and upon uniformity in the speed of the bow.

Rests and notes related to tension states in the arm. Staccato seen as a process of application and release of energy.

Vibrato seen as a function of the forearm and as part of a variable world of aesthetics. The three-fold division of the body considered.

Efficacy of practice dependent upon attention during analysis. The nature of attention.

The opposites as an intrinsic part of playing and of music in general.

Certain aspects of violin playing as a profession.

To claim that these concepts apply to all instruments would be extravagant, although the idea of player and instrument in itself can be said to give all instruments a common identity. The oboe player, the pianist and equally the conductor with his orchestra, are concerned with power, lightness, space, opposites and many of the principles with which this book is concerned: it is only that the particular application of the principles is necessarily different. It would not however be an exaggeration to say that they could be directly useful to players of any stringed instrument whatever, despite the slight differences in technical issues.

Few will dispute that the violin is the most complex of all instruments: yet behind the complexity lies a simplicity which awaits discovery. An attempt has been made to unfold the folds that hide this simplicity, and to relate them to the human being himself—for both are instruments of the utmost delicacy and can not be separated. If this book has in some measure, for some people, succeeded in doing this its purpose will have been realised.

FIN

INDEX